C000261409

Foreword by the
Keith White MA FRSA FCILI

Soon after Harry Wroe did me the honour of asking me to write this foreword I found my mind transported back to 1993 when the Society held its Annual General Meeting in Penrith. I stayed the night before the meeting at Derwent Bank and whilst looking for a book to read I found the first volume of the official history of the Society and soon found myself engrossed.

One of the things that brought to life the account of our earlier history was the inclusion of what became known to many as the "fed-up Charlie" letter. The unfortunate Charlie wrote his letter in the 1920s, but I think that each of us can relate in some way or another to what Charlie had to say. His letter reads as follows:

"Dear Alf

Your letter came along this morning asking me to try and book you up for next week if I thought this show was any good. Well, my advice is – keep out of it. There's about 80 people here and they're all mad except me. I'm not trying to be funny, old sport. I'm dead serious. Bar Sunday, it's nothing but hard work from the moment you've cleaned your boots in the morning and made your bed, until 10.30pm, when they sing something they call "No 95". Then the men go outside for a last smoke and the girls are shoo'd off to their dormitories like chickens.

These people are always singing, or trying to. They have sing-songs in the Common Room, and they sing on the hills when decent people want to have a nap. And when they're not singing in the evenings they do rotten plays by outsiders like G.B. Shore (I think that's the blighter's name) or else have round games or dances. They all seem to enjoy it! That's what licks me. But the limit came yesterday after an outdoor lunch of sandwiches mixed with grass and insects when some literary bloke started reading poetry aloud. Poetry! I tell you I'd pack up tomorrow only the Secretary collars your dibs on Monday night. That's where they have you.

And that's only half the story. What really gets over me is this passion for walking, wet or fine. As you know, I walked to the office twice last year during the railway strike without turning a hair, but that was on decent pavements and level roads, with plenty to look at. Here they walk up bally mountains and scramble through bogs and over slimy rocks. And when you get to the top there is nothing to see. Absolutely nothing but more bally mountains. Not a house in sight nor a human creature to speak to except your own crowd whom you're tired of.

What makes it worse is that men are expected to carry the lunch-bags, although many of the girls are as strong as horses. It's a good wheeze to leave your rucksack behind after a 'rest'. I brought it off yesterday. Then there's no billiard table in the house. You can't get a glass of beer without walking half a mile, and as for decent reading there's nothing but books about the open air. How I hate the words! Haven't seen the 'Daily Mail' since I came.

Well they say live and learn. I've learnt all right, but I'm half dead already. Anyway, it's Ramsgate again next year if I'm spared. Some lunatic has just shouted to me to join a party at the bathing pool at 6.30 tomorrow morning! I haven't answered so I hope he thinks I'm asleep."

Newfield Hall, Malhamdale

Not long after that, I was on a family holiday at Newfield Hall in Malhamdale. The swimming pool had not been built at that time but we were enjoying the pleasures of en-suite facilities, comfortable furnishings, the bar and good catering. In the corridor one evening, I met a lady in her 70s who was a long-term HF'er. She reminisced about the fun she had had in her youth when HF holidaymakers slept in single sex dormitories and helped with the washing up, before saying, "But of course, it's much better now!"

My own first holidays with HF Holidays were at a time when the product was well into the process of change from the one that Charlie knew in the 1920s. Yet it would still have been recognisable to my friend from Newfield Hall. We got wet, we got lost, we made evening drinks, we helped with clearing up, and we slept in a cabin-like room. After our first week at Milford-on-Sea we were completely hooked, and we have been coming back to HF Holidays ever since.

I wonder whether Charlie would recognise the world of walking as we know it today. In those days walking was a relatively inexpensive way of spending what leisure time people had. If you had stout footwear and warm clothing, you were ready to set off on a walk. Now, with the ever-growing and bewildering variety of specialised gear, we can find ourselves putting on several hundred pounds worth of clothing and equipment to take a walk in the country.

Please don't get me wrong: I love my waterproof boots, and my breathable, windproof and waterproof clothing, although I do sometimes wonder how any item of clothing merits the description "technical".

Real technology, in the shape of hand-held GPS devices and mobile phones, has provided us with new tools to make our walks safer. Of course, however, the fundamentals do not change, even if people's expectations do.

In January 2005, The Times carried the following report:

> "The distress call from the mobile phone of a couple stranded up a mountain in the Lake District sounded serious. 'We are lost in the mist,' said an anxious voice. 'My wife is very frightened. Please come and find us.' As the message continued, the mountain rescue team listened incredulously, 'And could you send a helicopter?' asked the caller. 'We have a dinner date at 7pm which we really don't want to miss.' "

Just as a person with GPS can state his or her exact position without knowing where they are, over-reliance upon mobile phones can lead the unwary into a sense of false security. A mobile phone is now one of the essential pieces of kit that a walker should carry, but it is no substitute for wearing the right clothes, carrying the right equipment and having a basic knowledge of the environment. As mountain rescuer Stuart Holles told The Times, "You need common sense and to treat the fells with respect. If you don't, then I'm afraid that a bucketful of mobile phones will not help you."

If Charlie were with us today, he might be the sort who would rather surf the Internet than share in the "passion for walking". Yet even there, he could log onto:

http://countrywalks.defra.gov.uk

and view a copy of a register of 2000 new walks along conservation area paths, all designed to welcome walkers into the countryside. He would find route descriptions and maps available online under the Government's Countryside Stewardship Scheme and Environmentally Sensitive Area Scheme.

It may seem a long way on from traditional black letter guides for walkers, such as Wainwright. In reality, however, it is only the medium of communication that has changed. The purpose remains as it has long been: to guide those who want to walk in the country and enjoy the open air.

So it is with our Society. It is a truism that no business can stand still. The business which does not move forward, inevitably falls backwards. HF Holidays has had a strong forward momentum throughout its history.

The Board and the Executive have repeatedly shown the ability to respond to market forces and I suspect that Charlie would be amazed if he were to come on one of our holidays now. En-suite facilities, no half-mile walk to get a glass of beer, possibly a swimming pool, consistently good catering and all that we have come to expect from a good Country House hotel. One thing that he would recognise is that he would have to go outside for a smoke!

He would also recognise the walking up bally mountains and scrambling through bogs and over slimy rocks. He would also recognise the pleasure and fun we take from the walks, the special activity programmes and the spirit of fellowship that is evident on an HF holiday.

As a business, HF must continue to look forward, but we would forget our history at our peril. Our history shapes our corporate personality, gives context to the way that we develop and informs our mission and purpose.

In the 21st century, HF Holidays continues to encourage and promote the healthy enjoyment of leisure, physical recreation and open air, with particular emphasis on walking (to use the words of paragraph 4.2.1 of the Society's Rules). Thus, we reflect consistently the ideals of simple-life holidays in areas of natural beauty that inspired T A Leonard to create this organisation in the early years of the 20th century.

Branksome House, Milford on Sea.

The Early Years

The beginning of the HF Holidays story is described in a book entitled *Adventures in Holiday Making,* written by Thomas Arthur Leonard. It was the only book he ever wrote and it was started in 1929 and finished in 1934.

T A Leonard was the Minister of the Congregational Church in Colne, north-east Lancashire, and this is where the idea of walking holidays started in 1891.

The inhabitants of this region were mostly hardworking mill folk and when the Wakes Week came round each year there was a general exodus down the long road to the station. The town well nigh emptied its population into the trains that carried them to Blackpool or Morecambe, with the more prosperous journeying as far afield as Douglas on the Isle of Man!

Leonard wrote, "This kind of holiday leads to thoughtless spending of money, inane types of amusement, and unhealthy overcrowding in lodging houses. Moreover it makes for perverse or corrupt conceptions of life and conduct, and produces permanent ill effects on character. Clearly the great majority of our young folk do not know how to get the best out of their holidays."

Thus a rambling club was formed and a holiday to Ambleside was planned in the summer of 1891. It ran for four nights from 13 to 16 June and this very first "HF style holiday" contained 30 in the party. It was to become an annual event. The second year the group went to Caernarvon, North Wales. In 1893 the venue was Keswick and for the next few years the group returned to this part of the Lake District where they enjoyed "basic accommodation".

Again quoting from Leonard's book, "In those days we were content with very primitive arrangements, so long as they gave us the joy and freedom of the open fells. All we needed was food, beds and good fellowship, and our quarters were a group of small houses at the top of Sanger Street, then a cul-de-sac in Keswick. The Leader for the week would trot round to each house during dinner with the announcements for the coming day. If he had a good voice he made them from the middle of the street, for we always lived with wide-open windows."

The first formal meeting of the group took place at Rivington Hall near Chorley in the New Year of 1894. At this stage there was no name and no constitution, but a committee was elected with Leonard as General Secretary. That year the charge for a week's holiday was 30/- plus 12/- train fare from Colne to Keswick or Ambleside.

1896 was a red letter year with the acquisition of the first property. This was Abbey House, Whitby, at the top of the famous 199 steps, on which a five-year lease was taken. By the end of the year, centres had opened at Portinscale, near Keswick, and on the Clyde near Helensburgh. Responsibilities were being created at such a rate it was decided to put the whole thing on a legal footing.

In 1897 therefore a small company was formed called the Co-operative Holiday Association – CHA. As a non-profit making organisation they were absolved from the use of the word "Limited" by licence of the (then) Board of Trade. That year, Leonard resigned from his minister's duties and became full time General Secretary with the headquarters at Abbey House.

By the end of the century CHA had six centres, at Whitby, Ardenconnel on the Clyde, Keswick, Barmouth, Hastings and Bangor. The business headquarters had moved to Ardenconnel.

During the first few years of the 1900s the organisation continued to expand with quite a few new centres being opened, two of which deserve a special mention – Keld in Upper Swaledale and Newlands in the Lake District.

Keld was opened in 1899 and only lasted three years. It was called a "Spartan" centre and the charge was 18/- per week. Water came from the village spring and there was no electricity. The only way of reaching the centre was to walk from Hawes railway station, some eight miles away over the Buttertubs Pass at 1,660 feet! The luggage was taken on a hand-cart.

Starting out on an excursion, 1901

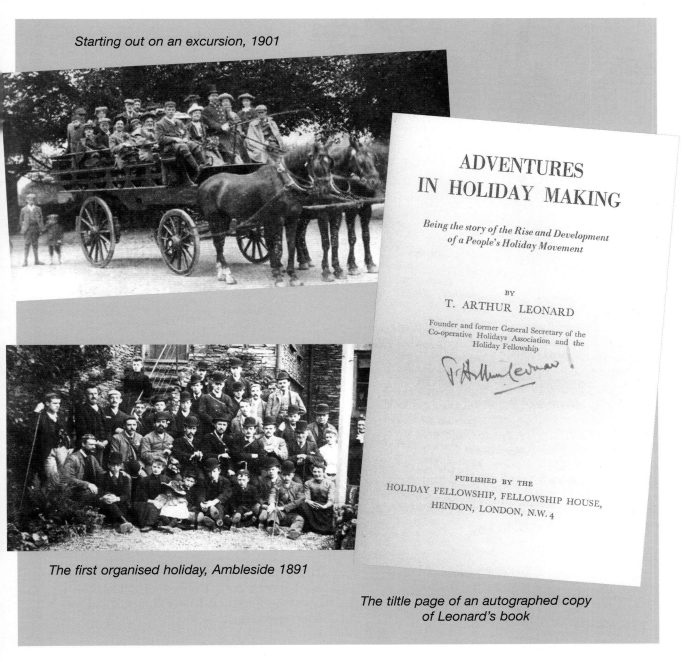

ADVENTURES IN HOLIDAY MAKING

Being the story of the Rise and Development of a People's Holiday Movement

BY

T. ARTHUR LEONARD

Founder and former General Secretary of the Co-operative Holidays Association and the Holiday Fellowship

PUBLISHED BY THE
HOLIDAY FELLOWSHIP, FELLOWSHIP HOUSE,
HENDON, LONDON, N.W. 4

The first organised holiday, Ambleside 1891

The tiltle page of an autographed copy of Leonard's book

Newlands (an old mill) was purchased in 1905 for £1,270, and, after extensive conversion, was considered "a place of sweetness and light". Just up the valley from HF's Derwent Bank it is still a holiday establishment today.

By 1913 CHA had grown to eighteen centres, four owned and the remainder on short leases, five of which were overseas. Over 16,000 guest weeks of holiday were sold, the turnover was £31,000 per annum and assets amounted to over £19,000.

However it was in 1913 that the idea of the Holiday Fellowship was first mooted. Leonard and a few friends felt that, despite working class origins, CHA had become rather middle class in spirit and conservative in ideas. They felt that the centres had become too conventional and had departed from the basic economic style. They also felt they were not making enough progress on the international scene.

So, with the goodwill and generous help of the CHA, the Holiday Fellowship was launched, going back to the original roots of simple adventurous holidays with the emphasis on youth. It was registered under the "Industrial and Provident Societies Act" so the word "Limited" had to be added to the title.

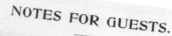

NOTES FOR GUESTS.

BRING WITH YOU—
(1) Bath Towel, as these are not provided ;
(2) Drinking horn for use at lunch. Paper drinking cups may be obtai
at the Centre ;
Serviettes are not provided at the Centre.
BOOTS.—Bring good strong boots, with low heels and soles thick enough to
hob-nailed. Boots can be nailed at Bryn Corach, price 4d. per pair.
BATHING.—The bathing place is near the mouth of the Conway. It can on
take place when tidal conditions are suitable, and when a rowboat is
attendance.
EVENING GATHERINGS.—Guests are asked to acquaint the Host or Hostes
if they can contribute to the interest of the evening gatherings, either with song
or otherwise. Good accompanists are always welcomed. There will be occa-
sional discussions upon topics of public interest. It may be helpful for guests to
inform the Host if they are disposed to open one.
The hour for retiring is 10-30, except on Wednesdays and Saturdays, when
the hour is 11 o'clock, to meet the wishes of those who desire to attend the
Llandudno concerts.

Programme & Time Table
FOR WEEKS BEGINNING ∴ MAY 22 ; JUNE 5, 19 ;
JULY 3, 17, 31 ; AUGUST 14, 28 ; SEPT. 11, 25.

MONDAY. 8-0, Breakfast.
Excursion : Marl Woods and the Little Ormes Head + + + Distance, 10 miles
Walk through the Marl Woods, and
return through Gloddaeth Woods and pass the remains of
Deganwy Castle.

TUESDAY. 7-15, Breakfast ; 5-30, Tea (at home).
Excursion : Moel Siabod Time : Ascent, 3 hours ;
Return, 3 hours.
Train from Conway station to Bettws-y-Coed. The height
of the mountain is 2860 feet, and the ascent is over a
good deal of boggy ground. Strong boots are essential.
From the summit the return route is along the ridge, and
so down to the road to Bettws-y-Coed, passing the Swallow
Falls and the Miners' Bridge.

A headquarters was needed and the current centre at Conwy, Bryn Corach, was purchased for £5,096. The Newlands centre, previously mentioned, was also acquired and the portfolio was completed with a house at Ingleton on the western slopes of Ingleborough in Yorkshire, and one at Portpatrick, on the Mull of Galloway near Stranraer. The centre at Kelkheim in Germany was transferred from CHA to complete the 1914 picture, and holidays started in Conwy in the Easter of that year.

Prices in the first year of the operation of Holiday Fellowship Limited were:

Conwy	32/6 per week + 4/6 for the walking excursions
Newlands	25/- per week
Ingleton	25/- per week + 3/6 excursions
Kelkheim	£5/10/6 per week or £8 per fortnight

If one slept in a "garden house" at Conwy (in reality a wooden shed) a reduction of 5/- per week was allowed.

1914 of course was not a good year to start sending people abroad, especially on a holiday to Germany, and it was inevitable that two guests who did not heed advice about extending their stay were interned for the duration. A four-year holiday for £8 was pretty good value for money, but the walks, although daily, would have been quite short!

However holidays in the UK continued during the Great War and some of the 1915 'Notes for Guests' make interesting reading.

The centre programme in those days also contained a song book, a practice that continued right up to 1933, and included such gems as:

In a prison cell I sat
Some time ago when funds were low
Come all you lads that wander free

…together with 140 other songs of all types – from hymns to spirituals and popular tunes of the day. No wonder Holiday Fellowship's guests were always singing.

One last story about the First World War and the Conwy centre concerned the practice of leaving the bedroom windows open at night. This caused the window blinds to wallop in the wind and, with a light on in the bedroom, it looked as if morse signals were being sent out towards the Irish Sea! More than once, armed men paid a visit and had to be convinced of our loyalty to the cause.

The Holiday Fellowship. P.229. GENTLEMEN'S GARDEN HOUSES. Conway Centre.

Our New Dining Room at Bryn Corach.

The Holiday Fellowship. P.228. LADIES' GARDEN HOUSES. Conway Centre.

Rag-Songs

Collected at various Centres of
the Holiday Fellowship between
1918 and 1930
by R.H.M. and V.F.H.

Published by
THE HOLIDAY FELLOWSHIP, LTD.,
FELLOWSHIP HOUSE, GREAT NORTH WAY,
HENDON, N.W.4.

Tel. Hendon 8011/2.

FOURPENCE

PRICE ~~SIXPENCE~~

(post free)

A.55.

HOLIDAYS

"FOR you who are looking forward to your summer holidays, I would urge strongly that without moral discipline nothing can be learned from nature. If you go into her presence unprepared she will either say nothing to you, or will respond ironically to your every mood. It you are about to visit some glorious piece of God's handiwork—sea coast or mountain—prepare for it as for a sacrament. Pray God to purge your minds from worldliness, self-indulgence, and vulgarity. Pray Him to give you the heart of a little child. Put your minds in tune with the holy ground on which you are soon to stand, God's temple, the floor of which is grass and flowers, and its roof the blue dome of the sky. Remember who it is that the living garment of God, the visible creation, half reveals and half conceals. Open your hearts to Him among the hills, as Christ loved to do, and put away all that is sordid and mean and impure."

W. R. INGE, in St. Paul's Cathedral.
July 13th, 1924.

(The above is published on a neatly printed card, by the Holiday Fellowship, Fellowship House, Great North Way, N.W.4.

Price, 6 Cards for 1d.—Post free, 1½d.

---

1 Fish-Balls and Bread.

Conway, 1920.

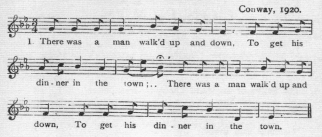

1. There was a man walk'd up and down, To get his dinner in the town;.. There was a man walk'd up and down, To get his dinner in the town.

2. And when at last he found a place,
He sat him down with modest grace.

3. He took his purse to count his pence,
And found he'd only five half-cents.

4. He searched the menu through and through,
To see what five half-cents would do.

5. And at the very end of all,
Saw five half-cents for one fish-ball.

6. He called the waiter down the Hall,
And softly murmured, "One fish-ball."

7. The waiter bellowed down the Hall:
"This gentleman here wants one fish-ball."

8. The people all turned round to see
Whoever on earth this man could be;

9. And then the man, all ill at ease,
Said, "A little piece of bread, Sir, if you please."

10. The waiter bellowed down the Hall:
"We don't give bread with one fish-ball.

11. "If you fish-ball with bread would eat,
You must bring friend to stand you treat.'

12. The next time this man dines in town,
He'll count his pence ere he sits down.

2 The Whale.

Newlands, 1918.

1. Did you ev-er, ev-er, ev-er, ev-er, ev-er, Did you ev-er, ev-er, ev-er see a whale? No, I nev-er, nev-er, nev-er, nev-er nev-er, No, I nev-er, nev-er, nev-er saw a whale.
2. Well, if you
3. For if you

2. Well, if you ever, ever, ever, ever, ever,
If you ever, ever, ever see a whale,
You must never, never, never, never, never,
You must never, never tread upon its tail.

3. For if you ever, ever, ever, ever, ever,
If you ever, ever, tread upon its tail,
You will never, never, never, never, never,
You will never, never see another whale.

3 Zimzamareebombahzooruzelladee.

Newlands, 1918.

1. Up-on a tree a Cuc-koo, Zimzama-ree-bombah-zoo-ru-zel-la-dee, Up-on a tree a Cuc-koo (shouted) SAT!

2. There came a cruel Hunter   FAT!
3. He shot that little Cuckoo   DEAD!
4. He shot it through its little   HEAD!
5. That night he ate the Cuckoo   ROAST!
6. Upon a piece of buttered   TOAST!
7. He found his beauty sleep was   SPOILED!
8. He vowed he'd have his next Cuckoo BOILED!

The Twenties

After the First World War HF continued to prosper and extend the variety of destinations both at home and abroad. In 1925 Altachorvie, the centre at Arran on a hill overlooking the waters of Lamlash Bay, was discovered. Remarkably it became the 74th centre opened by T A Leonard since the movement started as CHA in 1891 – obviously many of the other centres had fallen by the wayside.

The autumn of 1920 saw the introduction of a magazine called *Over the Hills.* Published twice or three times a year and initially priced at 4d per copy, it contained news and views of tramps (walks), climbs, books, holiday experiences, nature lore and expounded the ideal of international fellowship. There was a feature in each issue called "Intercepted Letters" and one of the earlier ones was as follows:

Altachorvie, Isle of Arran

"My dear fellow,

You ask for a few hints on the duties of a host ["Leader" in today's parlance] *and, as I am one at the moment (at least), they are fresh in my mind. Do not be terrified at the prospect, there is nothing to it. All that is required is tact, energy, a sanguine spirit, unselfishness, organising and entertaining ability, a capacity for doing without much sleep, keen observation coupled with a gift for not seeing things, a good memory and sense of humour, and above all a touch of humbug. A flair for sing-a-long songs – not music – is also a useful asset.*

Your first duty on the Saturday is to make the Manageress feel that you find her attractive. This will render the kitchen and larder accessible at all times. Next you welcome the incoming guests as if you had known them all your life, and desperately try to remember at least some of their names.

It should be an axiom with a host that guests are incapable of entertaining themselves. If, therefore, you see anyone not engaged in conversation, go to them without delay and start talking about crops, or the migratory instincts of glow-worms, or anything else that occurs to you. On the other hand, if two people are too much together, introduce a third. You can do no less.

Last to bed at night, you will make up for it by being first up in the morning, to deter jolly fellows from tramping about the house shouting as they go. In truth the biggest problem is to stop the guests linking arms and marching through towns and villages abreast. I have seen this at Keswick; innocent men, women and children – yes children – swept from the high street into shops, their faces frozen with terror.

As to complaints from guests about accommodation, food, the walks, or anything connected to the staff, agree with them every time. Say you will certainly enter them in your report to Head Office. Of course, you will do nothing of the kind but this will never come out, so all will be well. Your report, in fact, will be one long eulogy, "finest staff I have worked with", "best groups of guests ever", "really successful holiday" and so forth. This will ensure you being appointed as a host again and, after reading this letter, I am sure you will realise that the post is indeed a sinecure."

Some will say nothing much has changed over the ensuing years!

Centre Programmes

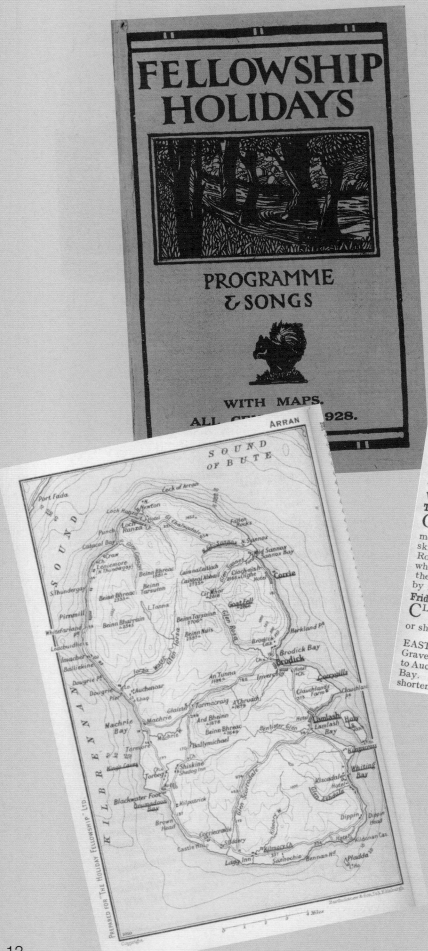

Each season HF published a bound collection of holiday programmes from all its centres, with maps and details of the walking excursions.

FELLOWSHIP HOLIDAYS

PROGRAMME & SONGS

WITH MAPS.
ALL CENTRES. 1928.

So brilliant was the landward view,
The ocean so serene,
Each puny wave in diamond rolled
O'er the calm deep, where hues of gold
With azure strove and green.

Programme of Excursions

AT LAMLASH, ISLE OF ARRAN, 1928.

Postal Address : "Altachorvie," Lamlash, Arran, Scotland. Telephone : Lamlash 23.

Weeks Beginning : May 26th ; June 9th 23rd ; July 7th, 21st ; August 4th, 18th ; September 1st.

Monday.

BEN LISTER GLEN AND GLEN CLOY.—Total walking distance, 10 miles. Route : Through the glen and over the moors to Brisderg, thence down Glen Dubh, passing the mounds believed to be the remains of Bruce's Castle, following stream to Brodick. Return by the old road.

Tuesday.

KILMORY, BY MOORLANDS.—Route : Through village and by-paths up to the summit of the moors, descending into Kilmory. Drive home along the coast, about 16 miles, passing Kildonan Castle and Whiting Bay. One-half of the party will work this journey the reverse way. This route can be shortened to 8 miles if necessary.

Wednesday.—Off-day. No Excursion is planned.

Thursday.

GLEN SANNOX AND GLEN ROSA.*—Walking distance, 9 miles. This is a fairly hard day. Take motor to Sannox Bay, thence track through the Glen, and skirting the peak Cirmhor follow the stream down Glen Rosa. Extension over Goat Fell after lunch. Those who cannot do this round will walk back to Brodick by the shore road through Corrie, 7 miles. Return to Lamlash by motor if necessary.

Friday.

CLAUCHLAND HILLS AND CORRYGILLS.—Route by road to Strathwhillan, returning either by road or shore. Walking distance, 8-9 miles.

OR

EAST MOR. Walk to Whiting Bay, thence to Giants Grave, via Glen Ashdale, and over Cnoc na Comhairle to Auchenhew Stream, and home by steamer from Whiting Bay. Walking distance 15½ miles. The distance can be shortened if desired.

Longshaw House, Derbyshire was acquired in 1915

In 1922 the price of *Over the Hills* was increased to 6d and there was much muttering and harsh words spoken. So much so that the following year the price was reduced back to 4d and there it remained until 1929 when it was once again increased by 50%. The Committee of the day pointed out that it was a "jolly good read" for 1/6 per year.

In the early twenties there was another interesting incident with a holiday group bound for somewhere in Europe. They described themselves as a jolly party travelling on the night train from Calais to Basle. After a lovely dinner in the dining car they were all tired and settled down, six in a carriage, for some sort of night's rest.

After midnight the Leader passed along the corridor to see that all were comfortable and, finding one compartment with the lights full on, all the others being in slumbering darkness, asked whether the travellers would not prefer the lights out. "We would," was the reply, "but we can't find the switch." After a hurried glance round, the Leader pulled a handle just inside the door. There was an instant shrill whistle and a sudden application of the brakes. Within half a minute, as the train came to a standstill, half a dozen worried officials appeared in the corridor simultaneously demanding, in French, who had committed the unspeakable crime of stopping "La Grande Vitesse". Calmly the Leader, in English, surrendered as the culprit, pointing out what he had done and why. With passion the chief official snatched a lady's hat hanging on a knob in the centre of the compartment, pointed dramatically to the knob as the proper thing to have been pulled, took out his notebook and demanded full particulars.

The Leader handed over his visiting card. This was closely scrutinised by each official in turn and they clearly doubted the validity of the document. "Where is Conwy?" they asked with emphasis. Then the Leader had a flash of inspiration – "La ville de Monsieur Lloyd George," he said, for was this not his constituency seat? Either the Leader's French pronunciation was not good or the name of David Lloyd George (who was very big in France in the 20s) set up a surge of emotion in their breasts. For an extraordinary change took place in the railway officials. They all lined up in the corridor, took off their caps, bowed to all the English party with faces wreathed in happy smiles, and murmured, "Les amis de Monsieur Lloyd George".

The Leader extended a dignified handshake, bows were repeated all round, and the incident closed. On reaching Basle, the railway officials all lined up on the platform with the local station staff, and the HF party were again wished "Bon Voyage".

Passenger to
The Holiday Fellowship Guest House
GRINDLEFORD STATION.
For
Longshaw House
Via L.M.S.
Name............

A Snowdon Party.   Mr. Jas. Daniel.
(Conway Centre.)

I stood tip-toe upon a little hill . . .—Keats.
Those who know Bryn Corach (and who of
the Fellowship does not?) will not need to be
told which hill-top from which we write. Our
" Dwarf Hill "—which is what the word mean
—holds no mean place in the affections of ou
Fellowship, so we have thought it fit to give
a place at the head of the column dealing wi
matters of central importance.

THE SEASON'S END.   We write amid th
mellow sunshine of one of these glorious day
of early autumn, when   Nature seems
to be trying to make ame
of rain and chilliness s
vious months.   The la
about to close, and we
seeing our own Fell
whom we invite and p
These will number o
range from 16 to 75.
will have!   Would t'
them arrive, then ha
mid-week, and finall
the last day of the
would be no lac
holidays..

MOUNTAIN TRAMPING—Manfield's are
asked by the Holiday Fellowship to recommend boots
suitable for this purpose.   The two examples are such.
Both made with Waterproofed (greasy) Russet Calf uppers
—a material which gives to the actions of the foot, and
is hygienic in wear.   Hard-wearing soles of suitable sub-
stance, not too thin to feel the rough places through, nor
too heavy to   make their weight un-
comfortably   felt after hours of tramping.   They are   of course only two of
the many boots   and shoes which Manfield's produce   for tourists.

No. LT 363
For Ladies,
39/9

No. MT 291
For Men,
32/6

Manfield
& SONS LTD

LONDON : 170, Regent St., &c.   MANCHESTER : 78-82, Market St., &c.
LIVERPOOL : 30, Church St., &c., and throughout United Kingdom.
Manufactory, Northampton.

A Hythe Party.

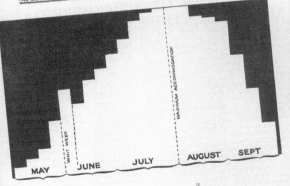

THE BLACK SPACES DENOTE UNUSED ACCOMMODATION WAITING FOR YOU TO FILL

MAXIMUM ACCOMMODATION

WHIT WEEK

MAY   JUNE   JULY   AUGUST   SEPT

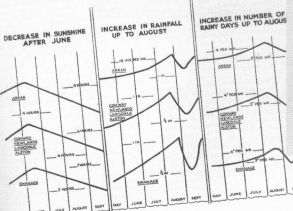

DECREASE IN SUNSHINE AFTER JUNE

INCREASE IN RAINFALL UP TO AUGUST

INCREASE IN NUMBER OF RAINY DAYS UP TO AUGUST

VIEWS · & · RE·VIEWS

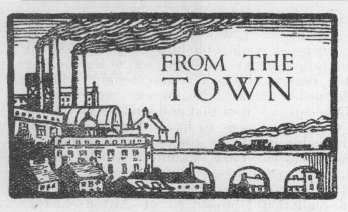

FROM THE TOWN

The Story of hf holidays

One other notable event was a meeting that took place in Conwy in 1924, when senior members of the Labour Party, chaired by Ramsay Macdonald, redrafted and redefined the Party's policies. A letter was published in *Over the Hills* No.12 in the spring of 1924 as follows:

From the Premier.

10, Downing Street,
Whitehall, S.W.1,
February 6th, 1924.

Dear Mr. Leonard,

I remember very well the restful and enjoyable time which we spent under the roof of Bryn Corach, and I have very much pleasure in sending you my greetings and best wishes for the success of the Holiday Fellowship. It is a splendid institution, and has afforded great pleasure to many people.—Yours very sincerely,

(Signed) J. Ramsay MacDonald.

By the end of the 1920s the Holiday Fellowship had 23 houses in the UK, three of which are still going strong today – Conwy from 1914, Arran from 1925 and Glen Coe from 1929.

Alltshellach, Glen Coe

Since 1914, when the Fellowship had 2,196 guests, there had been a steady growth in guest weeks every year, notwithstanding the First World War, and by 1929 the numbers had reached 28,306. A week's holiday at Conwy (in 1914, 32/6) had increased to 55/- by 1929, with the price of the excursions rising from 4/6 to 8/6 per week. As well as the UK houses, there were six European destinations in 1929 and the average charge was £15 for a two-week holiday, which included the train fare from London to the nearest station on the continent.

The Thirties

The organisation continued to grow steadily both at home and overseas. In the Christmas 1930 edition of *Over the Hills* there was a report on an HF Holiday Adventure to Leningrad, Moscow, Kiev and Rostov. The guests travelled on a clean, well-appointed and goodly ventilated steamer named the Co-operatzia.

In the same edition there were 68 associated walking clubs listed in the UK as well as four in Europe. The circulation of *Over the Hills* at that time was 21,000 copies and one of the features was entitled *Postbag*. There were letters and replies on all sorts of walking issues but one of the principle ones concerned ladies' dress on walks. Inevitably HF took the initiative and a pamphlet was prepared entitled *Dress Hints for Ladies.* This was strongly recommended and could be obtained from Head Office by sending a self-addressed pre-paid envelope.

Subsequently, dress hints for gentlemen became available, which were more or less the same as for ladies, with an additional item about neckties. "It is recommended that gentlemen sport a necktie for the evening meal and subsequent arrangements. This should be striped and most colourful so as to liven up the proceedings."

Much is made of food at HF and there was a debate about the right grub for mountain excursions. Dried bananas, with nuts and

Derwent Bank, on the edge of Derwentwater, became an HF centre in 1937

raisins, bitter chocolate and oatcake seemed to be in every mountain climber's rucksack. However hefty sandwiches of soggy marrow, jam or fish paste also featured.

Raymond Lambert, an HF Member and Everest climber, declared that his mountaineering diet was a large bowl of semolina pudding. Apparently he ate it first hot, then cold on all expeditions.

Another well-known Leader of the day, usually to be found at Conwy or Newlands, one John Ellis, had mountain legs marrowed with iron. His evening meal on the eve of tough excursions was nothing but bowls of rice pudding. His speed and energy were prodigious, frequently terrifying the guests.

Cliff House, Marske, HF's first family centre, opened in 1935

HOLIDAY FELLOWSHIP LIMITED
"Highfield," Golders Green Road. London, N.W.11.

Dress Hints for Ladies

UNSUITABLE dress deprives the wearer of much of the pleasure of our simple, unconventional holidays. When clothes are a discomfort and a nuisance to ourselves and others, we put a strain on the consideration of the hostesses and the chivalry of the men in the party.

At all Centres

Wear strong, low-heeled boots, woollen stockings; short skirt, close fitting hat or cap, in summer a light scarf or handkerchief for the head, a woollen jumper and light mackintosh or poncho.

A small rücksack or haversack is useful for carrying mackintoshes, scarves, etc., when not in use, and may be had cheaply from most local sports outfitters.

Complete changes of underwear, and plenty of woollen stockings are essential.

Guests are warned against undue exposure to the sun Boracic powder and cold cream are useful.

Simple evening frocks are quite suitable.

At Mountain Centres

Knicker-bocker costumes are recommended for mountain and moorland centres.

Boots are a matter of consideration on a tramping holiday, and the attention of guests is drawn to the following notes reprinted from *Over the Hills*.

Boot No 1 is what a novice usually comes in, and is hopelessly unsuitable. The soles and uppers are too thin, and as for the heels these tire the wearer, because they give no firm support to the foot. At mountain centres these heels come off by the score, and the boots are ruined before the week is out. No. 2 boot is a business-like article—low, straight, broad heels, giving good support, and thick soles with nails. The hefty boots marked 3 do not look lady-like, but, equipped as they are with climbing nails, are just fine for the fells and mountains. For ordinary tramps and climbs No. 2 are quite serviceable, No. 3 being designed for rocky climbs at home and abroad.

At the top of Dunkery Beacon, 1932

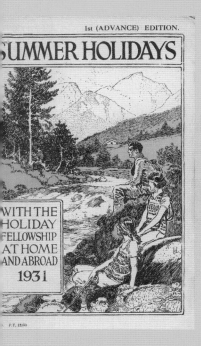

SUMMER HOLIDAYS

WITH THE HOLIDAY FELLOWSHIP AT HOME AND ABROAD 1931

1932

SUMMER HOLiDAYS BY Mountain, Moor & Sea.

ARRANGED BY THE HOLIDAY FELLOWSHIP
Fellowship House, Great North Way, Hendon, London, N.W.4.

'33

SUMMER HOLIDAYS

WITH THE HOLIDAY FELLOWSHIP
FELLOWSHIP HOUSE, GREAT NORTH WAY, HENDON, LONDON, N.W.4.

SUMMER HOLIDAYS 934

WITH THE HOLIDAY FELLOWSHIP
FELLOWSHIP HOUSE · GREAT NORTH WAY
HENDON · LONDON · N.W.4

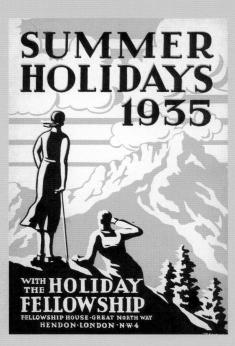

SUMMER HOLIDAYS 1935

WITH THE HOLIDAY FELLOWSHIP
FELLOWSHIP HOUSE · GREAT NORTH WAY
HENDON · LONDON · N.W.4

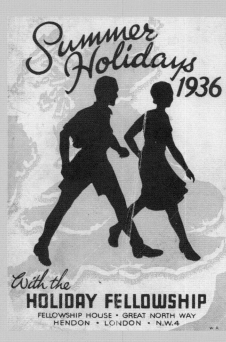

Summer Holidays 1936

With the HOLIDAY FELLOWSHIP
FELLOWSHIP HOUSE · GREAT NORTH WAY
HENDON · LONDON · N.W.4

SUMMER HOLIDAYS 937

WITH THE HOLIDAY FELLOWSHIP
FELLOWSHIP HOUSE GREAT NORTH WAY HENDON LONDON N.W.4

SOCIAL HOLIDAYS
AUTUMN WINTER & SPRING 1938-39

WITH THE HOLIDAY FELLOWSHIP
142 GREAT NORTH WAY HENDON LONDON N.W.4

SUMMER HOLIDAYS 1939

with the HOLIDAY FELLOWSHIP

There were a few rules at the HF centres at the time which today's guests might find interesting.

- At all centres except Hawes End, guests are expected to make their own beds and clean their own boots.

- At Alston, Froggatt and Newlands, guests will wait at table one day a week.

- At Devils Bridge and Langdale, duties also include preparing meals and washing up one day a week.

- No intoxicating beverages are allowed in the guesthouses of the Holiday Fellowship and guests are requested to refrain from their use on excursions.

Henry Stone

John Henderson

During 1931 the Watcombe Park centre near Torquay was opened. Designed by Isambard Kingdom Brunel for his own use, it was considered at the time to be the grandest centre owned by the Holiday Fellowship.

In 1933 Newfield Hall at Malhamdale was opened, which, after two fires and much repair and renovation, is one of the finest today.

Henry J Stone who took over from T A Leonard as General Secretary in 1926, died in his office at Fellowship House on 12 February 1934. He was succeeded by John Henderson, who held the post until 1950.

As mentioned at the beginning, *Adventures in Holidaymaking* was published in 1935, priced 4/6, as "The story of the rise and development of a people's holiday movement". In the same year Leonard was awarded the OBE for his services to the youth movement. (In 1930 he had been one of the prime movers in the foundation of the Youth Hostel Association.) Also *Over the Hills* was reduced in price to 3d and the frequency increased to four copies per annum, making a yearly outlay of one shilling, post free.

In 1936, at the AGM held at the De Montford Hall in Leicester, a motion was passed that "the General Secretary have discretion to provide a gramophone or a radiogram for the centres at Conwy, Lynmouth and the Wye Valley". This was a huge step forward, as the subject of "mechanical music" had been debated and rejected for many years. It had always been argued that young men and women fox-trotting to records was not in the proper spirit of the HF movement.

In all the centres, however, there had always been an extensive library, and this article appeared in the summer of 1937 in *Over the Hills*.

"There appears to be a steady leakage of books from the centre shelves. New books have disappeared within a few weeks of their arrival and only rarely does one return through the post. Can it be that guests, becoming interested in a book, take it to bed and then thoughtlessly take it home with the full intention of returning it – and then never do? This Leader was visiting a friend who had a fine library and, in looking through the shelves, spotted the face of a long lost friend. Automatically he looked inside the front cover and there was the tell-tale stamp. Should this paragraph reach the eye of this person, we shall be glad if the book is returned to the Manageress at the centre. We would also suggest that other friends might look through their shelves and do the same."

In the same issue there was a complaint of a different kind:

"As the season is approaching I want to utter a friendly remonstrance regarding the growing custom – especially at the strenuous centres – of our young stalwarts (of both sexes) disregarding the ways of decent society by coming to the evening meal not merely in their shirts and shorts, but with unwashed bodies. I know the Fellowship is not conventional in its ways but surely there are sanitary limits. And dare I mention another matter? I know it is risky but it is time the subject should be referred to. A few of the girls have taken to the nasty habit of lipstick. Some of them say it is because the boys like it. As a fellow, and knowing something of what the other fellows say, this is not so. It is often remarked that the girls of the Fellowship are nice precisely because they do not make up and adopt the ways of a decadent society."

At the end of the 30s there were 82 affiliated UK groups and two abroad groups, one in Germany and one in Kashmir. The number of guest weeks had continued to grow and had peaked at 45,169 at the end of 1938.

The 1939 brochure was very optimistic considering the growing political unrest in Europe. There were 44 centres (some of them short season) on offer in the UK and 33 destinations abroad, seven in Germany and

one to Poland and Czechoslovakia. Inevitably most of the European holidays did not take place and some of the UK holidays were also curtailed. Surprisingly the cost of a week's holiday at Conwy had fallen by 2/6 during the decade to 52/-, and two weeks abroad was just under £15.

The Second World War broke out on 3 September 1939. But already on 25 August Head Office had advised all Leaders at continental centres to return to Britain with their parties as soon as possible. There were immediate plans to close some UK centres and hand others over to the relevant government departments – some for evacuees, some for refugees and some for potential medical rehabilitation centres. Only Conwy, Crowlink, Derwentwater, Longshaw, Milford, Watcombe Park and Hitherwood were to remain open for normal business. Lynmouth, Penzance and the Wye Valley were to be opened if the demand arose.

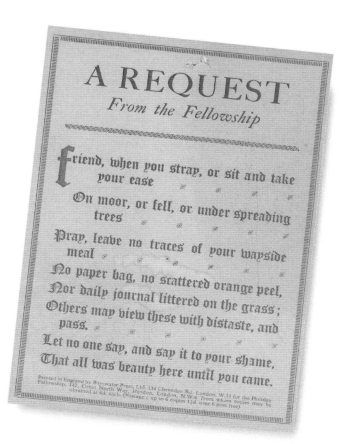

HF arranged for small metal signs like this to be placed in popular walking locations - an early example of concern for the environment

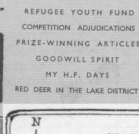

OVER THE HILLS
THE MAGAZINE OF THE HOLIDAY FELLOWSHIP

INCLUDING:

REFUGEE YOUTH FUND

COMPETITION ADJUDICATIONS

PRIZE-WINNING ARTICLES

GOODWILL SPIRIT

MY H.F. DAYS

RED DEER IN THE LAKE DISTRICT

G.B.S. AT CONWAY GUEST HOUSE

LEST our title should convey a false impression, we hasten to explain that George Bernard Shaw did not book at Headquarters months beforehand, that he did not sleep in a garden house, nor accompany the two day excursion to Snowdòn. The great dramatist, whose plays have filled the theatres of the world and whose ideas will be appreciated even more fully by a future generation, just " dropped in " to attend a Sunday evening discussion on " Crime and Punishment " at the invitation of the host, Edgar Chapman, and the Secretary, A. E. E. McKenzie.

Before venturing into our midst, however, it appears that he made most careful and personal inquiries as to our " respectability." To use his own words: " If you had been millionaires I'd have been damned if I'd have come."

We are indebted to Mr. Chapman and to Mr. McKenzie for the following account of this welcome visit.

Mr. Edgar Chapman, who met G.B.S. while out walking, writes:

" Remembering that G.B.S. was in the neighbourhood I recognised him at once. I went up to him, bade him ' Good morning,' gave him a welcome to Bryn Corach and asked could I show him round the Guest House of the Fellowship. He said he would be glad for he had never heard of the Holiday Fellowship. I told him I was surprised that most frien at h and from opir ther othe said

there and I don't want to put the authorities on you for overcrowding!!" I said, ' Come with me,' and I took him to the sun-parlour and showed him the garden houses which he thought were admirable. He asked about the origin of the movement and so I traced it for him from Keld to the present day. I tried to get in as much as I could. I summarised its Constitution, told him of our Goodwill Holidays and our catering for vegetarians. Told him we were not out for profit and he was astounded when I told him that three guineas covered a whole week with excursions. I explained how we arranged our evenings—our playreadings, talks and debates, outlined our Fellowship Service after supper on Sundays and finished by inviting him to come in ' tonight.' I said, ' We shall not make a fuss— you will be just one of us and, of course, if you like to say anything we shall be delighted to listen.' He seemed very interested and asked for some literature that he might send to a young friend whom he thought this kind of holiday would suit. I walked down the drive with him and off he went.

" After lunch I gathered some literature together and walked as far as the Oakwood Park Hotel. I produced my booklets, etc., and went through some of them. We chatted for three-quarters of an hour and discussed both drama and music. He was delightful to listen to and I really enjoyed myself. One was greatly impressed by his youthful bearing and

WHAT A VIEW! What country! What a place to rest! Out comes the Motoring Chocolate. Here's flavour and energy in a thirst-quenching combination of chocolate, nuts and juicy raisins. Every mouthful packed with stamina — it's the one best chocolate for any adventure and the Open Road!

*Tom Stephenson's original 193
proposal for the Pennine Way*

10   OVER THE HILLS

JOHN SHEET

"MR." SECRETARY   THE NEW STAGERS - AND - "THE OLD BRIGADE"

THE ATHLETIC PERSON - AND - ESCORT.   "THE WILLING HORSE"

"B" PARTY   THE AFTERNOON TEA EXPERT   THE RISING "BELLE"

FAMILIAR FEATURES.

A 137.   FIRST EDITION—JULY, 1932.

HOLIDAYS
Mountain Moor & Sea

During the
AUTUMN, WINTER & SPRING
1932~1933
ORGANISED BY THE
HOLIDAY FELLOWSHIP
FELLOWSHIP, HOUSE, GREAT NORTH WAY, HENDON, LONDON, N.W.4

Photo by Roy Dixon.

TRYFAN

Conway Centre.

THE GOOD COMPANIONS.

23

The Forties

The guest numbers for 1940 dropped dramatically to under 18,000 and, with further houses being requisitioned by the government, reached a low point in 1943 of 14,466. The financial turnover for that year was just £51,000.

Over the Hills reappeared in 1941 after several issues had been missed due to a paper shortage. Throughout the rest of the war, although quite short and printed on very poor paper, 28,000 copies per issue were printed and posted to the Members.

The spring of 1944 (issue No.72) saw the first mention of second-hand boots, a topic that was to rumble on for several years. It read as follows:

BOOTS: Nailed boots are a very necessary part of guests' equipment, but those not already in possession of these are apt to find considerable difficulty in obtaining them, not only on account of the expense, but also of the clothing coupon. Would any of our readers who have suitable part-worn boots, which they would be willing to be parted from for a consideration, send particulars of size and price to Fellowship House. Please DO NOT send the boots.

In 1946 the topic was still high on the agenda with this plea:

Requests for boots still outnumber offers for sale. It is requested that anyone having a pair of tramping boots or shoes that they are not likely to be using make the details available to Fellowship House where they will be redirected to a would be purchaser.

Monk Coniston, overlooking Conistonwater, opened in 1945

Nether Grange, Alnmouth, opened in 1947

On the subject of clothing coupons, the brochures during the war, and for quite a few years afterwards, advised guests that Ration Books, including full points for each week of their stay, must be brought by all guests.

By 1945 the brochure had reduced in size to a 6" x 4" booklet of eight pages with a few bits of scant information about location, closing dates and price. Guest numbers were increasing slightly as optimism returned and were just over 16,000. By autumn 1945 the Fellowship was receiving de-requisition notices in respect of the 20 centres that were being used by government departments. Most of them were returned in very bad condition and large compensation packages needed to be negotiated. Even then it was difficult to get tradesmen to effect the repairs and there were huge problems in subsequent years with lack of capacity to meet the renewed interest in walking holidays. In 1946 John Henderson was awarded the OBE in recognition of the social services of the Holiday Fellowship during the war years.

Holidays abroad were slow to get started in 1946 and only four parties of a limited size were planned for July and August to visit Norway travelling from Newcastle.

The Christmas 1946 edition of *Over the Hills* saw a return to the humorous items that had always been a feature of the publications before the war. There was a full page article describing the Perfect Host. It started thus:

At last we have found him - after years of patient waiting and stricken hopes. What a relief after suffering under the Host futile, the Host domineering, the Host facetious, the Host raw and the Host senile, to be led by the Host perfect.

It continued to describe the non-existent paragon and was followed in the spring 1947 edition with a response featuring the Perfect Guest, who on learning he was to be housed in the most distant garden house, made no complaint, but remarked on the compensations of the wide view from his window, etc, etc.

It was also reported at the Manageresses' Conference that concern was expressed over the increasing tendency for after hours bedroom parties. This was usually nothing less innocuous than a small number of guests, often with the Leaders, meeting together in a bedroom on a Friday evening to chat and sometimes sing together – though not always in tune – until around midnight. On the other hand at the AGM in 1947 concern was expressed that there was too much dancing at Christmas and not enough community singing!

1948 was a sad year for the Holiday Fellowship for it saw the death, aged 84, of its founder and first General Secretary, Thomas Arthur Leonard, at his home in Conwy on 19 July. Born at Stoke Newington, London, in 1864, he was considered by common consent to be the father of the outdoor movement in this country. He was an unorthodox radical who had many interesting ideas, typically trying to buy Mount Snowdon for the nation to commemorate George V's Jubilee. (The plan was rejected by the locals, who always thought there was *gold in them thar hills.*)

He was cremated at Anfield Crematorium in Liverpool and his ashes scattered in the rose garden there.

There was no charge made for *Over the Hills* after the war but copies were restricted to one per household, regardless of the number of Members who lived there. Each issue was eagerly expected and still considered a "jolly good read".

The 81st edition, which came out in the New Year of 1949, contained an article called *Gates I Have Closed* by Allan M. Laing. The pre-war standard of humour had definitely returned and it was followed in issue No. 82 with *The Reformer* by Mathew Weir about writing stiff letters to The Times. This, the author felt, was necessary but pointless, because he lived in Cheltenham instead of Tunbridge Wells or Basingstoke where disgusted or angry people generally hailed from.

One final item in 1949 was the introduction of the first "special interest" holidays. These were literature holidays at Cromer and Swanage and a music holiday at Bourton-on-the-Water.

The end of the 1940s saw guest weeks top 50,000 for the first time, with turnover up to £253,801 from a modest £50,000 in 1940. There were 34 centres in the UK and 18 destinations abroad, and the cost of a week's holiday at Conwy was 90/- for Members plus 2/6 for non-members, and the excursions cost 15/-. Two weeks abroad had risen to between £35 and £40 including rail fare. The brochure also reminded guests, "the simpler you dress, both in the daytime and evenings, the better," and that, "evening entertainment must close at 10.30pm and it is expected that all guests will be in their own bedrooms observing absolute quietness by 11.00pm."

The Fifties

John Edbrooke

Holnicote House, Selworthy

In 1950 John Henderson retired as General Secretary, a position he had held since 1934. His successor was John Edbrooke. In 1951 the death was announced on 22 May of Mr Arnold Rowntree aged 78. He had been President from the inception of the Holiday Fellowship in 1913 to 1923, from 1934 to 1937 and again from 1942 to 1946. In the other 19 years, and up to his death in 1951, he was Vice President.

By now the organisation had nearly 40,000 shareholders and one innovation for abroad holidays was the use of chartered flights across the Channel. There was much discussion about desirability of school and youth parties, which hitherto had been just about tolerated. It was realised that, without the financial advantages arising from accommodating this business, some of the centres would have to close. Accordingly, eight adult centres were given over to schools and youth parties, and new brochures published dedicated to *Education by Experience* which was the buzz phrase of the day. Needless to say, bookings increased substantially.

In 1951 a new songbook, *Songs of Faith, Nature and Fellowship,* was issued, sponsored jointly with CHA, soon becoming very popular. Priced at 5/6d for words and music, or words only for 8d, its preface urged host and hostesses to give community singing its due place in the social programme.

There was great debate that year on the subject of *Go As You Please.* Hitherto the policy had been one of compulsory participation in excursions, but the General Committee decided that the following year, as an experiment, the walks would be optional. There were articles for and against in the next

few issues of *Over the Hills*, but the argument prevailed that HF needed to know whether "undue regimentation" was putting people off.

This more relaxed view gave birth to another type of holiday. With the cooperation of the coach company, Royal Blue Express, five touring weeks to the West Country were organised in 1952. These were for people who wished to visit HF Houses but could no longer manage the walks. They were very popular, and eventually a Coach Tour brochure was produced to cater for these guests and the holidays ran independently for many years.

1952 saw two other events in the West Country. The first was the acquisition of Holnicote House at Selworthy, being the 33rd centre in the UK at the time.

The second occurred on the night of Friday 15 August just a few miles away at Lynmouth. It had rained heavily up on the moors for two days and that night an enormous flood of water came down the Lyn Valley causing devastation in the town. The HF centre there, the Manor House, was on the seafront to the right of the river as you look out to sea and was relatively undamaged by the disaster. But guests who were booked for the rest of the season had their holidays transferred to other centres and the house was immediately given over to the rescue effort. Many local people stayed there free of charge for the rest of the year, and the whole facility was placed at the disposal of the police and the authorities.

T A Leonard had died in 1948 but it wasn't until the early 50s that a memorial was agreed upon and established. There are in fact three plaques as reminders of the great man's work: one on

The Manor House, Lynmouth

a rock face just below the summit of Cat Bells above Derwent Water; a second which was originally near the summit of Conwy Mountain, is now re-sited on a wall in the grounds of Bryn Corach. The third is in an acre of gorse and bracken-covered rock, about 500ft above sea level on the eastern side of the River Conwy opposite to Dolgarrog. The site adjoins the little village of Maenan and bears the name Cadair Ifan Goch (Red Ifan's Chair). It was Leonard's favourite spot in North Wales, with a splendid view of the mountains of Snowdonia, and is approached from a small car park adjacent to the now closed Maenan School, a walk of about 20 minutes. After his name and brief details of his life, the plaques all bear the

inscription "the best things any mortal hath, are those which every mortal shares".

The front cover of the summer holiday brochure of 1953 was the first to be in colour. That Christmas staff gratuity boxes were introduced in all the houses for the first time. The practice was subsequently discontinued, and then reluctantly re-introduced in the late 70s. It was to be finally confirmed at the AGM in 1981. Sometimes Holiday Fellowship does take a while to make up its mind! Also in 1953 it was agreed as an experiment to attach the dinner menu to the notice boards at the centres.

memorial plaque
Cadair Ifan Goch

THOMAS ARTHUR LEONARD
FOUNDER OF CO-OPERATIVE AND COMMUNAL HOLIDAYS
AND FATHER OF THE OPEN-AIR MOVEMENT IN THIS COUNTRY
BORN LONDON MARCH 12TH 1864.
DIED CONWAY JULY 19TH 1948.
BELIEVING THAT "THE BEST THINGS ANY MORTAL HATH
ARE THOSE WHICH EVERY MORTAL SHARES" HE ENDEAVOURED
TO PROMOTE JOY IN WIDEST COMMONALTY SPREAD

The view across the Vale of Conwy

Poetry while you walk

GLASBURY

1952

Dancing on Glasbury Station while waiting for the train home

Occasionally Over the Hills would print poems sent in by guests or Leaders, describing their holiday experiences. Here are two from the 1950s.

OVER THE HILLS   *Spring Number*

THE STATION THAT LIKES TO BE DANCED ON

By W. STEWART

(At Glasbury-on-Wye, it has now become the established custom for Tregoyd guests to dance on the station platform on Saturday mornings, before taking the 11.8 train to Hereford. This has made Glasbury internationally famous.)

This Glasbury-on-Wye must not
   Be ranked with other stations:
It is unique; for, once a week,
The people on the platform seek
   The gaiety of nations.

While elsewhere passengers complain
   Of late trains, with impatience,
We take the chance to start a dance
And add a little gay romance
   To Brecon's reputations.

The stationmaster's gramophone
   Attends on our vacations,
When waltzes, reels, on toes and heels,
Strike from the concrete rhythmic peals
   Which earn us loud ovations.

Look round, now, on the photographs
   That picture these occasions:
See thus employed guests from Tre-
   goyd,
By lightest hearts and spirits buoyed:
   Hail! happiest of stations!

From Over the Hills Spring 1954

R THE HILLS   *Christmas Number*

I WONDER WHY?

By C. N. BROOKER

I wonder why the sky is always bright when duty calls,
But when I lead a ramble, it is then rain always falls:
   Or if the sun is shining, and my mac I should forget,
The weather changes suddenly from dry to ' very wet '.
         I wonder why?

I wonder why the pleasant paths—those carpeted with grass
Are on the route through which MY rambles never seem to pass:
   And why it is that others on their walks find all the flow'rs,
But only thorns and brambles grow so thick and strong on ours.
         I wonder why?

I wonder why, untiringly, I'll dance the eightsome reel,
Yet, when I lead a ramble, must get blisters on my heel;
   And why the ground walked over with such ease the other week,
Turns to a virgin jungle, through which un-mapp'd paths we seek.
         I wonder why?

I wonder why the tea-place that I choose is always shut,
Which, when we're tired and thirsty, seems a most unkindly cut:
   Or why it is, at journey's end, the train has just gone out,
And when the next is due to leave is open to such doubt.
         I wonder why?

And so I often wonder why, when things like this go wrong,
Or else I lose the way and take a route that's twice as long,
   My party thank me nicely and from finding fault refrain,
And always say " We liked it " and " I hope we go again ".
         I wonder why?

Reprinted from " Sou'wester."

Roger Bannister

It was noted at the AGM in 1954 that Grosvenor House, Scarborough, had just been purchased lock, stock and barrel, including a full set of teapots – HF have always got their priorities right! Also in 1954 Roger Bannister broke the world mile record recording the first sub four-minute time of 3 minutes 59.4 seconds. The Bannister family were committed Fellowship folk with his mother and father giving considerable service as Host and Hostess and his sister on the domestic staff.

Roger himself was a Centre Secretary and his involvement went back to his days as a young lad at Marske by the Sea in 1937.

There was an excellent article in the 95th edition of *Over the Hills* called *Gentleman's Privilege* by John Battersby. The subject was the custom of gentlemen waiting on the ladies for Sunday tea and thereby missing out on all the choice cakes! His practice was to secrete some items behind the curtains before the ladies arrived. If he was observed, he developed a tactical limp which usually had the ladies waiting on him! John was at it again in the 99th edition with two items on offer. He took first prize in the literature competition with a serious poem, but his feature called *Answer in the Negative* was awarded first prize in the *Articles* competition and was pure joy. It concerned a group of photographers of the serious kind on holiday with HF. Here's an extract:

"Their accoutrements hang about them in such profusion they look for all the world like the

members of some vague but desperate guerrilla organisation, and one imagines the secret kit inspection that takes place somewhere round the back of the guesthouse before the party moves off. Cam-er-aah... Open! Spring release in the off position, film loaded, flaps down... Get that lens cleaned, it's a disgrace! Check all your buttons: lens hood, lens filter, red filter, yellow filter... Tripods at the trail position: Quick March!"

In the summer of 1954 the coach tours were extended to Scotland and there was another holiday on offer to get north of the border. Coast Lines of Liverpool operated cruises to the Scottish Lochs, the Hebrides, and round the coast of the British Isles. It is recorded that the holidays were much appreciated, but not much walking was possible.

Also in this year the last of the government hostels under HF management was closed and

Grosvenor House, Scarborough

warm approval expressed by the Minister of Labour and National Service for the invaluable help given by Holiday Fellowship over a long period. In November 1955 the General Committee (today's Board of Directors), clocked up their 400th meeting since the start of operations in 1914. In the Minutes, complaints about talking and singing by early morning staff on duty were countered by criticism of guests singing in their early morning baths! It is not recorded whether the complainants were other guests or the early morning staff.

At the AGM in 1956 an item was first debated that is still raised today: that the name "Holiday Fellowship" was off-putting. Another matter of concern was that between 15 to 25% of new guests experienced the holiday once and then did not return.

HOLIDAYS
WITH THE
HOLIDAY FELLOWSHIP
SCARBOROUGH

Hosts, Hostesses, Secs and Staff

The Bannister family were fairly typical in providing both Leaders and staff for HF, and a word of explanation is needed about how this worked in their day. Up until the end of the Seventies the team of Leaders were made up of a Host (male), a Hostess (female, often married to the host) and a Centre Secretary (usually abbreviated to "Sec"), who could be either. There was no official training for any of these people. They were simply sent a booklet describing the various things they were to do: lead the walks, arrange evening entertainment, make announcements, serve late-night "drinkables", compère the Concert, provide First Aid, and so on.

Usually the Centre Secretary (who also took the balance of the guests' payments on a Monday, and their excursion coach money on a Friday) would lead the longest walk (the "A" party) each day, but didn't help with the evening entertainment. Many "Secs" would be at the House for two months or more, often students on summer vacation, and they received a small honorarium.

The Host and Hostess in contrast would be there only a fortnight at the most, and were unpaid. They led the shorter "B" and "C" party walks, but were responsible for the social programme. To assist with this they would choose a "House Committee" of four volunteers from the guests. It was from these volunteers that future Hosts and Hostesses were usually recruited.

The domestic staff were also part of this network of self-help. Many of them were students, or girls from abroad wanting to learn English. Their wages were modest, but their hours not so long as today. They were encouraged to join in the evening social programme when they'd finished their duties, and were allowed to go on one walking excursion each week on their day off. Sometimes they'd also appear (as might the redoubtable Manageress) in the group photo. This was taken by the photographer each Monday morning, and put on sale to the guests later in the week.

One of the big challenges for any walking Leader, whichever party he or she takes, is to find the most appropriate spot for lunch...

"A" Party

"B" Party

"C" Party

Freshwater Bay House, at the foot of Tennyson Down on the Isle of Wight, was purchased in 1956.

In the winter of 1956 Malhamdale was opened at a week's notice to accommodate Hungarian refugees, and in early 1957 a second group were taken in at the youth centre at Kessingland, near Lowestoft, under the auspices of the British Council for Aid to Refugees.

A new brochure appeared in 1957 called *Autumn, Winter and Spring* which outlined holidays outside the main walking season. Meanwhile *Over the Hills* had grown to 36 pages and a charge had been re-introduced (9d with postage free).

The autumn 1958 edition featured a piece by Mrs A M Vanstung entitled *The Authentic History of the Holiday Fellowship.* She traced the beginnings right back to the Stone Age where primitive woman badgered primitive man to take her and the primitive kids to a *Gust House* for the holidays – usually on the edge of a cliff and so called because it was always very windy. She continued the history through the Romans to Ethelred the Unready, a great walker but who kept missing the bus, William the Conqueror, Sir Francis Drake, Charles II, Nell Gwyn and the Duke of Monmouth, all apparently great HF people. She concluded her piece, "considering our beginnings, it is not surprising that some of our customs and much of our behaviour is a little primitive".

1959 saw the publication of the first brochure dedicated to 'special interest' holidays entitled *Holidays that are Different.* These included Pony Trekking at Glasbury, Riding at Cromer, Golf at Conwy, and Geology Study at Arran and Loch Leven. The indoor activities included Photography at Cromer, Art & Sketching at Torquay and Longshaw, Scottish Country Dancing at Marske-by-the-Sea and Minard, and Old Time Dancing at Torquay. There was also an intriguing holiday entitled "Music While You Walk" at Coniston and Conwy. Close scrutiny of the programme indicated that the vocal element of the holiday took place in the House after the morning walk. The cost for all these holidays was between £8 and £9 per week, with an extra £2 on the Golf Holidays to cover green fees.

Guest numbers during the 50s had remained fairly constant at an average of 60,000, with a choice of 32 adult centres plus 8 youth centres in the UK and 48 destinations abroad.

Our yardstick on prices, Conwy, had risen to £9/12/- per week with £1 extra for excursions. A reduction of 10/6 per week was made if you were in a garden house and the charge of 2/6 for non-members remained. The European tours for two weeks varied between £30 and £50 depending on destination and air or sea travel. The most expensive on offer was a six and a half week holiday to New York and the Eastern Seaboard sailing via Montreal, which cost £195 plus an advisory note to take £50 in American money for incidentals such as afternoon tea! By 1959 HF had doubled the 1949 turnover to over £500,000, and the surplus generated that year was £13,134.

We'll Meet Again

Beginning in 1951 (and for the next two decades) one of the major events of the HF year was the Grand Autumn Reunion in the brand new Royal Festival Hall (built to celebrate the Great Exhibition of that year) on London's South Bank. No-one quite knows how HF managed to book this prestigious venue, though it seems that the Manager might have been a Member.

Throughout the summer, Centre Secretaries would sell tickets in the Houses, and then on the first Saturday in November HF-ers from all over Britain would gather in their hundreds to re-new acquaintances. Each centre was allocated three rows in the concert hall so that people could meet up easily, and they would then enjoy a mixture of concert items, slide shows and dancing, and partake at the bar. Rumour has it that the bar takings on the HF Reunion evening were always the highest the Festival Hall achieved throughout the year - somewhat puzzling for an organisation that would not countenance bars at its Houses!

AT THE ROYAL FESTIVAL HALL
THE FELLOWSHIP'S AUTUMN REUNION, November 3rd, 19...

This annual fixture in London has been a feature of the Fellowship's "off-season" programme for over twenty years. One recalls during that period happy gatherings at the Central Hall and the Horticultural Hall in Westminster, and at Friends' House, Euston. This year, however, we aspired to the Royal Festival Hall on South Bank.

It proved to be a magnificent setting for our purpose, and the air of excitement and enthusiasm engendered will long be remembered by all who were present. No doubt curiosity to see the Royal Festival Hall was a factor in the attendance of over four thousand, and in there being a considerable number of applications which could not be accepted owing to the booking capacity of the Hall having been reached several weeks before the date of the Reunion.

had. The spacious foyers, galler... staircases round the buildin... Lower Foyer where dancing too... and the Meeting Room where a... entertainments were provide... excellent for the different uses... they were put, and there is li... that every individual in... attendance felt that he or sh... ceived more than full valu... money. Everything went... or at any rate very nearly...

Following Community Sir... ably led by George Hill... Hart at the piano, the sp... Fred Dodson presiding... Chorley and Mr. David H... listened to in a crowde... and the General Secreta... ary on lantern slides... centres was very much e... tiful ciné films in col... transparencies (for the...

IN THE CONCERT HALL

6.30–7.15 p.m.	Conversation.
7.15–8.00 p.m.	A Short Talk by the General Secretary, a Community Song " Riding Down from Bangor," followed by a Display of Coloured Slides covering many Fellowship Centres, concluding with " Jerusalem."
	Community Singing conducted by George Hill.
8.00–8.15 p.m.	Conversation.
8.15–9.00 p.m.	National Folk Dancing Display by a team from Morley College Folk Dancing Club led by Charles Rowse, including English Folk, Sword and Morris Dances. Music by Helen Farrow, at the piano, and Martin Jolley, on the violin.
9.00–9.30 p.m.	Conversation.
9.30–10.15 p.m.	" Music in Miniature," presented by George Hill.

King Charles ... ... Maude Valerie White
The Lute Player ... ... Frances Allitsen
TOM EGBEARE

TRADITIONAL SCOTS SONGS
Lewis Bridal Song ... ... Grieg
Air Falalalo ... ... arr. Hugh Roberton
ELIZABETH MUIR

Silent Worship ... ... Handel arr. Arthur Somervell
Hugh's Song of the Road ... Hugh the Drover ... Vaughan Williams
DONALD WYNN

Art Thou Troubled? ... ... Rodelinda ... Handel
The Silver Ring ... ... Chaminade
MOLLY COLLINS

ENGLISH AYRES
What Thing is Love? ... ... John Bartlett arr. Frederick Keel
My Thread is Spun ... ... Anon arr. Peter Warlock

ENGLISH FOLK SONG
Nutting Time ... Suffolk ... arr. E. J. Moeran
GEORGE HILL
At the Piano—MOLLY COLLINS

The Fellowship's Autumn Reunion, Royal Festival Hall, London, Saturday, November 3rd, 1951. In the Concert Hall. (Photo by John Bold.)

The Sixties

For the next few years the financial performance was not so good, but the average number of guests throughout the sixties continued at over 60,000, peaking in 1963 at 67,744 which, incidentally, was the Jubilee Year for the organisation.

Mr J Battersby of Harrogate was at it again in the autumn 1960 edition of *Over the Hills*. This time he had turned his attention to the tremendous expansion in far flung destinations dreamt up by the Long Term Planning Committee (LTPC) who he suggested sat in permanent session on the tenth floor of Fellowship House in Hendon. He mused that the LTPC were probably planning trips to the moon or even further afield. He foresaw a problem in setting off for, say, Saturn as a sprightly youth, for you would be in the Old Stagers club by the time you got there, and would therefore have packed inappropriate walking gear. A lateral thinker was our Mr Battersby.

In the early sixties it was agreed to request guests not to smoke in the dining rooms, and try and reduce the practice in the other public rooms.

1962 saw significant centre changes with the acquisition of The Fold, a hotel in Stratford on Avon, so called because it had been owned by the Lamb family, and The Beaconsfield, a hotel with 100 beds in Newquay. By then Longshaw House in Derbyshire had gone after 32 years and the end was in sight for Ballycastle in

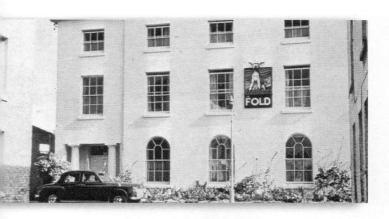

The Fold, Stratford on Avon

Belvedere House, Colwyn Bay

Ireland (34 years), Watcombe Park in Torquay (32 years) and Kessingland after 26 years. In 1963 two more properties were added to the portfolio – Belvedere House, a hotel in Colwyn Bay with 100 beds, and the Resthaven Hotel in Devon, subsequently renamed Thurlestone Sands House.

As mentioned before, 1963 was the 50th anniversary of the Holiday Fellowship and notable milestones that year were: one and a half million guest weeks sold since 1913, and collections for the Goodwill Fund topping £90,000, from which over 30,000 people had enjoyed a free or assisted holiday.

The mid-60s were a period of consolidation throughout the organisation with the abroad holidays not achieving their expected growth due to intense competition from the "package deal" operators. Italy was the most popular country for HF visitors at this time but the most popular centre was Ehrwald in the Austrian Tyrol.

At the 1966 AGM in Scarborough two recommendations in the Annual Report were rejected. It had been proposed to change the names of the *Quiet Room* and *Common Room* to *Lounge* and also to discontinue saying a Christian "grace" before meals. Although the votes were narrowly lost, it showed that a clear wind of change was blowing through the Society.

Goodwill & Pathways

"Goodwill" Fund began as the social conscience
e Fellowship, and was providing free or assisted
ays long before the coming of the Welfare State.
n Sunday evening in every HF House, guests were
ed to contribute to the Fund. Then, usually in the
mn, special "Goodwill" holiday weeks were
nised at a number of Houses by local voluntary
mittees. The programme would be like a
ern-day "Rover" holiday – more sightseeing and
as much walking as the guests could manage,
always with a full social programme. Any Member
d nominate a person they thought would benefit.
only proviso was that he or she should not have
n on holiday for the previous three years. Here's
one Member recalls her Goodwill experience
the early sixties.

n I was in my late teens my Saturday job was
ing on the forecourt of the local filling station.
osite was a terrace of rather old, dingy cottages,
I soon became aware of the "little old man" who
utside one of them on a kitchen chair every day,
lly in his slippers, watching the traffic go by. It
't take me long to realise that he had no friends
mily to visit him, no outings to make, and so was
lonely. His name was Cyril, and he would often
ure across the road to join me on the forecourt,
ly to have someone to talk to.

amily had introduced me to HF in the womb, and
d listened to "Goodwill" talks and contributed to
collections on all our family holidays over the
s. Of course I knew nothing of Cyril's personal
umstances (he revealed little about himself when
ame over for our little chats) but I was certain that
ody deserved a free holiday more than he did,
I asked his permission to nominate him.

I have to admit, as I filled in the form, I was unsure
how he would get on. He clearly wasn't up to the
usual walking and dancing that I'd done on HF.
But I needn't have worried. For Cyril was accepted,
and as I saw him off at Leeds station on his journey
to Scarborough I knew he was simply looking forward
to being with other people. When he returned a week
later there were tears of thanks in his eyes, for he'd
quite literally had the time of his life.

From the 60s onwards there was a marked fall
in the number of nominations because of economic
and social changes, like the provision of outings by
Social Services and other charitable organisations,
the development of the cheap package holiday,
and a general increase in prosperity.

By the 1980s it became difficult to spend all the
money raised, but there was now a recognition of
the threat to the environment posed by the huge
increase in leisure walking. Paths were suffering
from erosion, particularly in those areas where
HF guests walked most, and maintenance budgets
for stiles, field boundaries and footbridges were
under increased pressure.

So over the last 15 years the emphasis of the
Fund has altered, with more money given as grants
to footpath work. Two examples are the provision of
new stone steps and kissing gates in Lathkilldale,
Derbyshire, and the work to improve the footpath
on the Waterfalls Walk in the Upper Neath Valley,
South Wales. To recognise this, the Fund was
renamed "Pathways" in 1998, and so far has made
grants totalling £270,000 in locations all over
the country.

The Beaconsfield, Newquay

Also in 1966, UK and abroad holidays were combined into a single brochure which contained coloured pictures inside for the first time. It ran to 96 pages but was still A5 in size. 1968 saw the introduction of the A4 size that we have today and that year's School and Youth Party brochure was the first to be published in colour throughout.

There were restrictions on taking money abroad in the 60s which limited the holidaymaker's expenses to £50. The dreaded "V" form had to be filled in for each holiday and HF calculated that the average abroad holiday would take £25 of these expenses, leaving a sum "adequate for the full enjoyment of the holiday".

The 1968 AGM held at Leeds spent a considerable time discussing cooks – or the lack of them at some centres – and food. It was decided to introduce *convenience* foods into 19 houses, some extensively and some partially. The view expressed was that, with cooking problems in mind, this represented the greatest breakthrough for our catering staff in 20 years. There was no subsequent record of what the guests thought, but the decision was reversed within a few years.

Early morning tea was also introduced as a "self-service system from facilities at strategic points in relation to bedrooms" – in other words a trolley with a large teapot and cups and milk. Guests would emerge from their bedrooms in a variety of nightwear with dishevelled hair to get their early morning cuppas from the trolley, and were expected to leave 6d per cup as a sort of tea fairy!

At the AGM in London in 1969 there was a motion "that all guests over 60 years of age be excluded from mountain centres". As there was not a seconder the motion was lost. But a more significant series of proposals were carried, which were the beginning of big changes in attitude and ideas. It was agreed that at three centres (Coniston, Marske and Newquay):

1. *No organised excursions would be laid down.*
2. *Led walks would be offered only if requested.*
3. *Go As You Please details, maps etc would be available.*
4. *The Common Room/Quiet Room would be renamed Lounges.*
5. *A bell would not be rung before mealtimes.*
6. *Grace would not be said.*

In addition it was agreed that there should be a major change in the presentation of our publications, with the accent on enjoyment, not restrictions and that the term House Party Holidays should be used rather than Guest House Holidays.

There was also further discussion about the 'Holiday Fellowship' name and a competition was set up to find an alternative using the HF initials. In spite of a prize of two week's holiday and an amazing number of replies, the judges felt that nothing submitted was acceptable. It is a pity that there is no written record of these entries but some ideas have drifted down through the years, such as: Husbands Found, Holidays Formidable (the French version), Hills and Fells, and Holidays Forwalkers (all one word). Maybe the judges were right!

Thus ended the 60s. The turnover in 1969 was £709,546 compared with just over £500,000 ten years before. One week's holiday at Conwy in the summer season was now £14/17/- per week (up from £9/12/-) with £1 extra for a single room and 30/- extra per person for a room with a bath. Excursions were up to 25/- but the Garden House option was no more – these had been replaced by a new wing. The average cost of two weeks abroad including flights was £60-£70.

ABROAD

HOLIDAYS **ABROAD** 1961

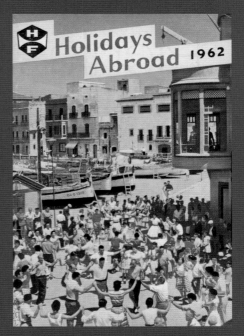

Holidays Abroad 1962

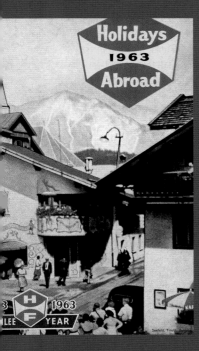

Holidays 1963 Abroad

1963 JUBILEE YEAR

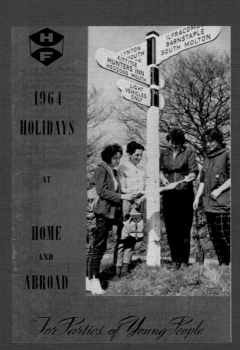

1964 HOLIDAYS AT HOME AND ABROAD

For Parties of Young People

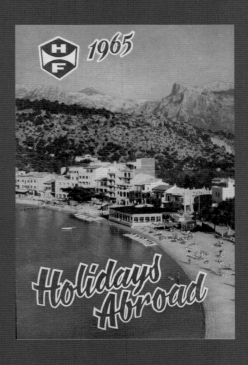

1965 *Holidays Abroad*

HOLIDAYS IN BRITAIN ABROAD 1966

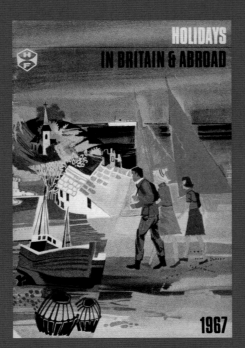

HOLIDAYS IN BRITAIN & ABROAD 1967

THE HOLIDAY FELLOWSHIP Ltd

SCHOOL AND YOUTH PARTY PROGRAMME 1968

Picnics, Packed Lunches & the Lettuce Rucksack

Over the years the provision of lunchtime sustenance to HF walkers has gone through a number of changes. Until the early 60s there was no ready supply of paper bags (fish and chips were wrapped in yesterday's *Daily Mail* in those environmentally unconscious days). So the various components of guests' lunches were carried "wholesale" in a number of official HF rucksacks.

For each walking party, A, B and C, there would be: a sandwich rucksack (you usually got one meat and one jam, but all made with ARTOX pure wholemeal bread to guarantee "an unclogged system"); a cake rucksack, with a great slab of fruitcake on a tray and a large knife for the Hostess to cut it; and, on hot summer days, a lettuce rucksack.

"Fed up Charlie" noted at the start of our story how unwary male guests found themselves carrying these, and it was the lettuce rucksack which was the least popular; for in those pre-clingfilm days there was no way of preventing the freshly-washed contents dripping down your back!

When the lunch spot was reached (often a farmhouse garden), the local Doris Archer would dispense a welcome cuppa into a medley of chipped crockery, and the contents of the rucksacks would be distributed, rather like the Feeding of the Five Thousand.

One drawback of the system was that it didn't allow guests to change their minds after breakfast about which walk to do. If you'd signed up for A party, then your sandwiches would be in the A party rucksack. If you opted for a shorter walk (or stayed in the House), you starved!

The advent of cheap paper bags revolutionised the system overnight. Now it was possible to provide an individual service, with guests choosing their sandwich filling, and self-selecting other items. But there was an initial reluctance for this largesse to be open-ended. "You may choose SEVEN items" was the rule (five for lunch, two for tea), and eagle-eyed management were often on hand to prevent abuse: children pocketing three packets of crisps and four "Mars" bars were always smartly dealt with!

Today the free market reigns, the choice can be quite out-facing, and the temptation to *over select* dangerously strong. So as we face up to the Age of Obesity, maybe a return to the regime of the lettuce rucksack would have its advantages!

The Seventies

In the early 70s there was a recession and guest bookings did not increase as had been expected. Fifteen years previously there had been talk of 100,000 guest weeks per year, but the only growth in the 70s was with youth holidays and school children. The centres used by these groups were easy to maintain (lots of wooden huts) and always yielded a financial surplus.

In 1972 John Edbrooke retired as General Secretary of Holiday Fellowship and the position was taken over by Michael Carter who had been his assistant for nine years. John Edbrooke was always thinking of making HF that bit special, and he strove to maintain the integrity inherited from its founder. At the same time he recognised the need to be flexible and expand to meet changing conditions. He had been at the helm since 1950.

At the AGM it was agreed to provide free flasks of tea and coffee with packed lunches, but only on request.

1973 was the Diamond Jubilee Year for HF and there were many special holidays, reunions, celebrations and rallies commemorating sixty years of Fellowship. One notable holiday was the visit of a group of Irish children, from both denominations, to the centre at Towyn, supported by the Goodwill Fund.

The introduction of VAT in 1973 caused much confusion to everybody, but created a windfall for HF as most people, in order to avoid the new tax, paid for their holiday that year embarrassingly early, producing a hugely advantageous cash flow. Added to this, the membership topped 70,000 for the first time and the turnover for the year came very close to £1m.

The mood and style of *Over the Hills* had changed over the first few years of the 70s. There were now mostly serious articles on the past performance and future prospects of HF. There were no competitions, humorous anecdotes or poems. Mr J Battersby of Harrogate had hung up his pen. There were, though, lots of features and advertisements about Special Interest holidays at home and abroad. In fact if you were reading the magazine for the first time you would have assumed that was what HF was about – walking was seldom mentioned. On a lighter note it was spotted that one of the destinations in Europe in 1974 was Adelhorst (near Fussen in Bavaria) which is, in fact, an anagram of Aldershot!

Netley House, Gomshall, leased from the National Trust, offered walks in the Surrey countryside and sightseeing tours of London

As these two views show, the station in the grounds of Loch Awe House was well patronised.

The mid-70s were difficult years for the whole country. There was industrial unrest and inflation neared 25%. In 1975 the published charges could not be maintained and a surcharge of £2 per week was added to each holiday. It says much for the tolerance and understanding of HF guests that this announcement was received with hardly a murmur.

Also in 1975 the "rising bell" was finally discontinued in all houses (prior to this a member of staff had patrolled the bedroom corridors every morning, 45 minutes before breakfast, wielding a small hand-bell). This caused problems with people missing breakfast, so an alternative was quickly put in place which became known as *New Gongs for Old Bells*.

The next year's accounts showed an item of £36,874 to cover dilapidations following the decision to end the lease on Netley House, the centre at Gomshall in Surrey.

Also in 1977 inclusive rail tickets with holiday costs were introduced with special fares for HF customers to all parts of the country. All parts, that is, that Dr Beeching had left connected! One of these destinations was the superb new house at Loch Awe in Scotland, acquired in 1974. The station, on the scenic line to Oban, was within in the hotel grounds and was re-opened almost exclusively for the benefit of HF guests.

1979 saw HF once again coming to the rescue of less fortunate people when the youth centre at Hythe was given over for 18 months to accommodate Vietnamese Boat People.

During the 70s *Over the Hills* increased in price first to 10p (new money – remember the country had gone decimal in 1971 so that was 9d to 10p). And then in 1978 it doubled to 20p. It was now filled with adverts about holidays and personal reminiscences, with the odd poem for light relief. Not surprisingly, when the quality of paper it was produced on deteriorated, the end was in sight and 1983 saw the last edition. The *jolly good read* had begun to reflect the pessimism of the times, for the 70s had seen the closure of the centres at Lynmouth after 50 years, Marske after 40 years, Glasbury after 32 years, Gomshall after 28 years and Aberystwyth after 22 years.

By the end of the decade, guest weeks had fallen to 52,000, but turnover, due to increased prices, was nearly £3m. Our week in Conwy now cost £66, £82 if you included the rail fare from London. Excursion costs had risen to £5.50. Two weeks abroad by air was now between £300 and £350 and two weeks in the USA on the Appalachian Trail was £582. The *Holidays that are Different* brochure contained nearly 150 special interest holidays, including some abroad, a huge increase over the previous decade.

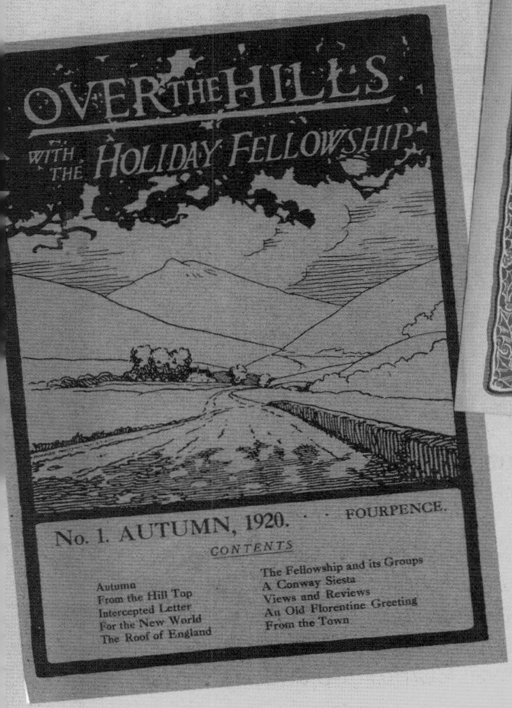

OVER THE HILLS
WITH THE HOLIDAY FELLOWSHIP

No. 1. AUTUMN, 1920. · FOURPENCE.
CONTENTS

Autumn
From the Hill Top
Intercepted Letter
For the New World
The Roof of England

The Fellowship and its Groups
A Conway Siesta
Views and Reviews
An Old Florentine Greeting
From the Town

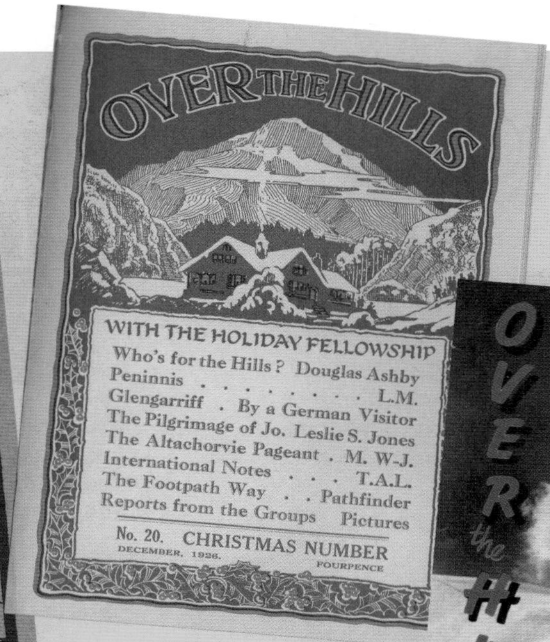

OVER THE HILLS

WITH THE HOLIDAY FELLOWSHIP
Who's for the Hills? Douglas Ashby
Peninnis . . . . L.M.
Glengarriff . By a German Visitor
The Pilgrimage of Jo. Leslie S. Jones
The Altachorvie Pageant . M. W-J.
International Notes . . . T.A.L.
The Footpath Way . Pathfinder
Reports from the Groups Pictures

No. 20. CHRISTMAS NUMBER
DECEMBER, 1926. FOURPENCE.

OVER the HILLS

CHRISTMAS 1958
Volume 2 No. 5
THE MAGAZINE OF THE HOLIDAY FELLOWSHIP

A selection of covers from the 62 years of Over the Hills

OVER THE HILLS

THE MAGAZINE OF THE HOLIDAY FELLOWSHIP

SPRING 1950 · No. 84

HF
Over the Hills
Volume 2 No.18

H.F. HOLIDAYS
*
Tell your friends about them
*
SPRING 1965
THE MAGAZINE OF THE HOLIDAY FELLOWSHIP

OVER THE HILLS
HF
SPRING '76

Including Autumn, Winter and Spring Holidays '76/77

The Eighties

Trem Enlli, Towyn, was first used in 1946. Situated on the seafront, near the boating, tennis, putting and swimming facilities, it was a very popular family centre.

1981 was not an easy year, due to unemployment, short working time, and the growing competition from the abroad holidays sector of the industry. However, the year saw a number of innovations, particularly that of the "£3 rail ticket" offer, which produced a record number of bookings to the remoter centres.

The biggest problem was a fall in adult guest weeks during the peak season, which followed a similar fall in the previous year. This meant that a number of centres were half empty during the peak summer weeks.

This trend continued into 1982 and, although turnover was up to £3.5m, the company again recorded a financial loss. The position was slightly improved by the sale of the house at Towyn *(Trem Enlli)*.

It was decided at the 1982 AGM to revise the name of the company from 'Holiday Fellowship' to simply 'HF Holidays'. Another motion debated was that "this meeting is of the opinion that locks and keys need to be provided for guests' bedrooms at all HF Holidays' guesthouses." Mr H Marshall, on behalf of the General Committee, explained that the cost of providing locks and keys would be more than £12,000, and although there was some value in the suggestion, he felt that it was not a sufficient priority to justify the expense. Other Members contributed to the discussion, and after a vote, the motion was declared lost. No locks and keys! Today's guests would be absolutely mortified at the idea. But one important change was approved: the introduction of bars at three centres for an experimental period.

Also during 1982, HF appointed marketing consultants who recommended the production of five different holiday brochures with branded names ('Wayfaring Holidays', 'Hobby Holidays', 'Young World Holidays', 'Harmony Holidays' and 'Holidays Abroad'), enabling selective attacks to be made on various market sectors, and making it easier to deal with the specific requirements of new guests.

There had always been a close relationship and friendly rivalry between HF and CHA, and at the AGM in 1983 at the Bloomsbury Crest Hotel in London there was a motion aimed at the possible merger of the two organisations. It read as follows:-

> *"The Fellowship, considering the financial results of recent years, and more particularly the change in pattern of holiday making, resolves that the General Committee should:-*
>
> *(a) face the desirability, if not the necessity of coming together with our forebears, CHA, to build a new organisation with fewer Houses, in order to maintain for the foreseeable future the great traditions we have both had in the past.*
> *(b) approach CHA immediately so that they can, at their meeting in three weeks time, discuss this issue, hopefully to approve the principle, then:-*
> *(c) proceed in both organisations, eliminating those difficulties which exist, to create this new organisation by the end of 1986."*

After lively debate the motion was lost, but a second motion was carried as follows:-

> *"That in the event of an approach being made from CHA with a view to a merger, this Annual General Meeting urges the General Committee and the General Secretary to take all steps to ensure that a constructive and business-like approach be given to the ensuing discussions."*

Thus began a long debate which was to continue for almost ten years!

Something Special

Throughout the 1950s there was the odd mention of alternative types of holiday in the main walking brochures, but the first brochure dedicated to Special Interest Holidays, entitled 'Holidays that are Different', appeared in 1959. It was quite a modest A5 size booklet in black and white, but it soon gave rise to tales of strange birds spotted in even stranger places, and outstanding performances on wind swept golf courses.

For instance there was one dedicated lady golfer from the north of England who travelled by public transport to the remote centre at Cromer. This involved five changes of train, and at each station she would throw her golf clubs out on to the platform first. This would be followed by a heavy suitcase, a grip, her handbag and finally an umbrella. But she clearly thought the exercise worthwhile, for, successful or otherwise on the links, she returned to play golf at Cromer every year for the next eighteen years!

During that time the programme had grown substantially and included Music Making, Bridge and, perhaps surprisingly, "Car Maintenance for Beginners" at the Stratford on Avon centre, which was a hotel slap bang in the centre of the town, with no garage or parking!

By 1983 there were 126 different 'Hobby Holidays' on offer from 28 different UK centres. All the traditional ones that are popular today were now included, but "Car Maintenance" had fallen by the wayside.

Two years later the brochure was extended to cover special interest holidays abroad: the Pyrenees for Botany, the Swiss Alps for Photography, Brittany and the Cote d'Azur for Landscape Painting, and best of all the Champagne Region in France and the Rhineland of Germany for Wine Appreciation. Note that it had only been three years since it was agreed to allow intoxicants to be consumed at just three of the UK Houses. Perhaps this latest "Special Interest" contributed to the decision to take a more liberal view on alcohol, for very soon there were bars in most of the Houses.

Throughout the 1990s the range of activities was continually refined and updated. As the popularity of one holiday declined there was always another to take its place, and there was an increasing emphasis on the opportunities for couples or friends to enjoy different holidays at the same time, for instance one guest doing landscape painting while their partner went walking.

In 2000 the title of the brochure was changed to 'Creative Britain' which was supplemented in the autumn of 2002 with 'Walking and Special Interest Breaks'. This was aimed at highlighting the short break off-season opportunities for guests wishing to pursue their favourite hobbies or pastimes. Since 2003 the programme has been entitled 'Inspirations', and is recognised as one of the best of its type on the market today, with over 500 different holidays on offer at home and abroad.

I wonder if that's the last trump?

YES!

HOLIDAYS

That ARE Different, 1959

Michael Carter

Also at the AGM it was reported that the Chief Executive and General Secretary, Mr Michael Carter, had undertaken Church Ministerial training, and been accepted for ordination by the Bishop of St Albans. He was now seeking early retirement in order to devote all his energies to a pastoral Ministry, and would relinquish his post towards the end of 1984. He had guided HF Holidays for 12 years, maintaining its unique appeal in the face of growing competition from the overseas package industry, and he has continued to serve the Society to the present day as an enthusiastic Vice President.

Peter Brassey

To seek a replacement for him, an announcement was made in the 1983 issue of *Over the Hills*, and the post was also advertised in national newspapers. Mr Peter A Brassey was appointed Chief Executive (Designate), and took over responsibility for most of the day-to-day operations. During the overlap period he also concentrated on a review of the administrative structure at Head Office, and introduced a number of changes to strengthen the marketing and promotion effort.

During the next couple of years more of the unprofitable centres were sold. The Hythe youth centre and the Crowlink centre which had been making considerable losses over a number of years, were put up for sale in 1983, and sold in 1984. The centres in Stratford-upon-Avon and Llandudno were also closed at the end of the year and sold in October. Other youth centres were reviewed, and Snowdon was sold to the existing manager in September. The lease for Devil's Bridge was also surrendered at this time and taken on by the existing managers.

Moyle Tower stood on the seafront at Hythe in Kent. Opened in 1923 it was closed during the war being a bit near to a potential invasion. From 1963 to its closure in 1983 it became a dedicated youth centre, aptly suitable for the purpose, with room for 90 guests.

North Barns, Crowlink, less than half a mile from the Seven Sisters cliffs. One of the current walks from Abingworth passes this spot.

Dorchester House, Llandudno another seafront centre.

Substantial financial losses continued into 1984. These were times of radical realignment both in terms of the packaging and marketing of the product, and of administrative and financial infrastructure.

The year commenced with a reduction in the number of brochures by combining the 'Wayfaring' and 'Abroad' publications. A Guest Report Form was introduced and, based on comments received, it was clear that the great majority of guests, once they had arrived at a centre, enjoyed happy and very satisfactory holidays.

Spending on capital improvements during the year remained low in view of the financial position, but a major refurbishment of Freshwater Bay took place, and central heating was installed at Loch Leven. The licensing operation was extended with the installation of bars at Derwentwater, Freshwater Bay and Loch Leven.

Despite a the poor start to the year, the main summer period showed an underlying trend upwards, indeed during the main holiday period the majority of centres were fully booked, and even into September they were all very busy. Thus the overall number of guests for the year remained static.

1985 was the year when the fortunes of HF Holidays started to run again in a favourable direction.

A comprehensive review of the HF's offices had been completed and its operations restructured, and the trend of increasing financial losses had been arrested.

The closure of older and less popular centres, (Cromer was sold in February and Newquay before Easter) had resulted in a substantial improvement in occupancy of the remaining centres. In the summer period particularly, HF maintained, and in some areas increased, its level of bookings and all centres showed a marked increase in profitability.

There was a substantial investment in bespoke accounting software. In addition, the introduction of payment for holidays in advance of arrival resulted in a substantial simplification of the cash handling process at centres. Over the previous three years the youth operation had also been reduced by four centres, with consequent cost savings, and in

October 1985 the youth centre at Llandogo, in the Wye Valley was sold. The operation at Newlands was reviewed and it was decided to invest substantially in improvements to the decorations, toilet and washing facilities and equipment. A refurbishment also took place at Newfield Hall, the youth centre in Malhamdale, involving considerable redecoration. These capital works resulted in a profitable well-run, well-maintained set of properties contributing to the work of HF Holidays in the provision of good value accommodation for young people.

Link Side, Cromer was situated on the outskirts of the town near the golf course, whence came its name

The Priory, Llandogo

HF's Youth Centres

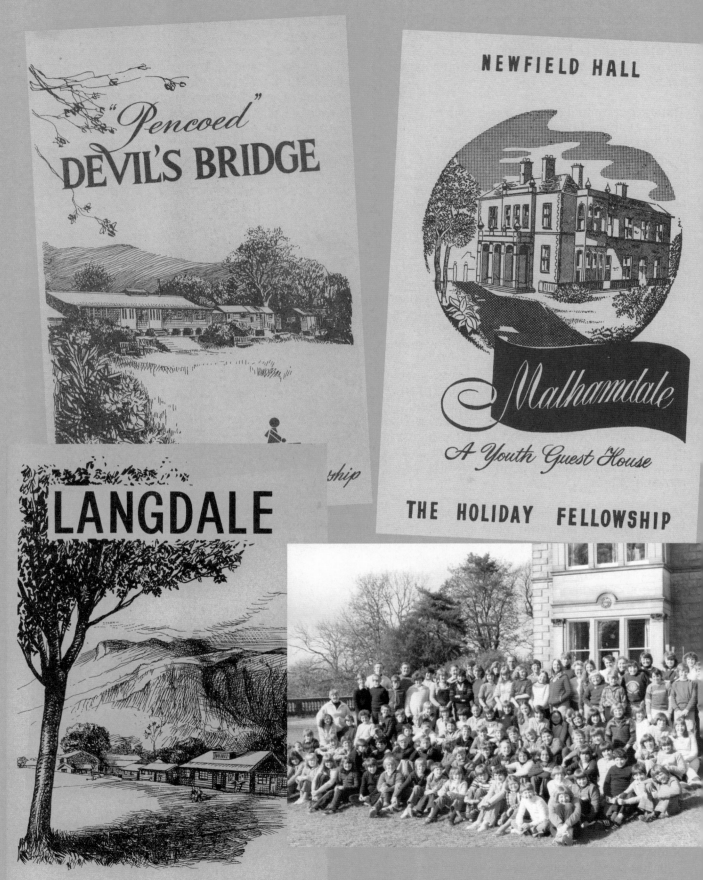

"Pencoed" DEVIL'S BRIDGE

NEWFIELD HALL

Malhamdale

A Youth Guest House

THE HOLIDAY FELLOWSHIP

LANGDALE

THE HOLIDAY FELLOWSHIP

WYE VALLEY

The Holiday Fellowship

NEWLANDS
A YOUTH GUEST HOUSE

THE HOLIDAY FELLOWSHIP

Hythe

THE
Holiday Fellowship

Ponsandane, Penzance

In 1986 a new property was purchased to replace Ponsandane in Penzance, which had been blighted by a new by-pass for the town. This was the Chy Morvah at St Ives which gave Members an opportunity to continue their acquaintance with this delightful area of Cornwall. Arrangements were also made to renew the lease for Monk Coniston, and it was planned that this House would be extensively renovated during the following eighteen months.

The move to a "flexible" breakfast time in the Houses (it had been fixed at 8.30 hitherto) was universally popular, and staff found that, with some spacing of demand, service was not quite so hectic and more time was available to meet guests' requirements.

The provision of more vegetarian meals at dinner was similarly popular and at times as many as 30% of guests were taking the opportunity to sample these, usually with very positive reactions.

Some new holidays were also introduced in 1986.

Fellowship Weeks, aimed at the "senior citizens" amongst the membership, offered the true spirit of friendship in relaxed Country House surroundings, a special tradition of the organisation. Entirely optional gentle walks and rambles through lovely countryside, coach excursions and social activities were all part of the programme.

Walks of Discovery were especially interesting to those who enjoyed Mike Harding's talks on BBC radio that summer. They combined the pleasure of walking with a special interest – natural history perhaps or industrial archaeology. For the experienced walker, 16 of the great walks of Britain were featured in a series of holidays which were called *Long Distance Walks,* including the arduous Pennine Way and the beauty and charm of the Cotswolds Way.

Occupancy levels improved during peak holiday periods, but there was a disappointing start to the year due to poor weather, a decline of interest in Scotland and industrial action in schools. This meant the bookings overall were down on those of 1985.

In 1987 a new company logo was implemented throughout HF and substantial funds were channelled into a campaign of advertising and public relations. The success of this was unquestionable and resulted in a noticeable increase in the number of new faces in all the Houses that year.

After an exhilarating walk over the hills, and a bath or shower, the guests are ready for one of the highlights of an HF holiday, the evening meal, and just minutes before the appointed hour, an orderly queue usually forms near the dining room door.

Signs of the times

Not surprisingly, the new company logo in 1987 wasn't the first or the last change, for the HF letters have appeared in a variety of styles over the years.

1925

1939

1950

1961

1973

1987

and today

hf holidays
better walking altogether

Balmoral Lodge, Strathpeffer lasted 40 years from 1947 to 1987, when it was closed, as popularity in Scottish holidays dwindled.

However, demand for holidays in Scotland had declined and Strathpeffer, as the weakest of the four Scottish properties both in location and construction, was sold in December. The programme was consolidated into the other three Houses, which resulted in increased occupancy levels in the Loch Awe and Loch Leven Houses. Further funds were applied to Arran to continue its development, and single chalets were converted to en-suite. Arran then had 17 single rooms, a very high percentage of the total capacity compared with many of the other Houses.

For some time the shareholding structure had been cumbersome and excessively costly to maintain. Of the 84,000 shareholders nearly 40,000 had only a £1 share; many had moved or lost contact with HF. The Special General Meeting in Glasgow that year authorised an increase in minimum shareholding to £25 for new Members, and existing shareholders were asked in the membership mailing either to increase their holdings to the new minimum figure, or to donate their shares. As a result of this mailing nearly 17,000 shareholders donated their shares and just under 8,000 increased their shareholding to the £25 figure. That still left 30,000 Members that never did reply.

During the year a decision was taken to lease offices in Penrith to accommodate those functions which could be operated successfully away from London. Walking operations, hotel services, staff recruitment and surveying were moved there. Initially the offices were in the town but two years later they were relocated to a renovated farm building on the outskirts.

At the AGM in 1988 it was announced that the President had decided to retire. Mr Peter Boulter had been president of the Society since 1983. His 5 years in office had seen very many changes in almost all aspects of the Society. He was retiring to follow other demands upon his time, mostly professional, but also to finish off his 'bag' of Munroes.

He was succeeded by Mr Keith White. Both he and his wife were Members of HF and had taken a number of family holidays. At the time he was Corporate Secretary of the Crown Agents for Overseas Governments and Administrations (a statutory corporation engaged in International trade providing services to the developing world).

For the summer season HF contracted a hotel for sole use at Le Bettex, St Gervais, near the Chamonix Valley, with an outstanding view of Mont Blanc, the highest mountain in Europe. Holidays were to be available for 7 or 14 nights, with the choice of arranging one's own transport to Le Bettex, or booking an air flight through HF. Although subsequent holidays abroad did not have sole occupancy, many of the aspects of Le Bettex provided a blueprint for the future.

Guidelines for Success

The 80s saw big changes in the way HF Holidays recruited its walking Leaders, and a story from the late 70s illustrates why these were necessary.

It concerns a Host at Loch Leven, who had decided to busk with his bagpipes by the Ballachulish Ferry rather than look after his HF guests. He was promptly dismissed by the Manageress, who then asked one of the more outgoing guests if he would organise some entertainment during the evenings for the rest of the week. This he did, and on the Saturday as he left he was given his money back! Head Office then wrote to him and asked if he would be willing to become a Host, and in fact he remained a Leader for 30 years and was still organising riotous evenings up to Christmas 2003. So the story had a happy ending. But it highlighted the growing shortage of good Leaders that HF Holidays was experiencing.

The old system of personal recommendation was no longer sufficient. In particular the falling level of university grants meant that very few students could now afford the luxury of a (virtually) unpaid holiday job. So in 1985 the Walking Department at Penrith was established, and the whole system of identifying and appointing Leaders (who would be called simply this, no longer Host, Hostess or Secretary) was changed.

Prospective new Leaders now filled in an application form giving personal details including their walking experience and leadership skills. They also needed the support of two sponsors. Those selected then attended a weekend course in the middle of winter at either Monk Coniston or Derwent Bank where HF's best Leaders acted as assessors, and applicants were tested on all aspects of becoming a Leader. These included navigational and interpersonal skills, party management and the ability to cope under pressure. One of the sessions took place outside at night, where in January in the Lake District, with no street lights and no moon, navigating by compass was as challenging as in a thick mist on a mountain top!

On these first courses more applicants were rejected than accepted, but the result was a rapid rise in the size and quality of the Leader panel. Since then, *Guidelines* (as the assessment is now called), has changed significantly, and pre-assessment filtering has increased the 'pass' rate to around 60%.

Here the Leader is addressing the potential hard or high level walkers

Here the easy group eagerly await their turn

On successfully completing their course new Leaders are given an authorisation of between 'B' and 'F', depending on their technical ability, stamina, experience etc. Leaders authorised as 'B' can lead at low level Houses such as Bourton-on-the-Water and Abingworth, while an 'F' Leader can lead in the highest Scottish mountains.

To maintain a panel of over 800 voluntary Leaders there are now up to seven Guidelines courses each year and candidates come from a variety of backgrounds including doctors, gardeners, teachers, civil servants and postmen. Probably the largest single category is retired police officers. Unfortunately, there are still significantly fewer women than men on the panel, and with the decline in early retirement in recent years recruitment is an ongoing challenge.

There is a similar programme and recruitment procedure for Leaders for abroad holidays, with the added requirement of a knowledge of one or more foreign languages.

Also in 1988 changes in schools' requirements informed the decision to withdraw from the operation of youth centres wherever possible. Accordingly the youth centre at Staithes was sold in July. This was a property consisting of wooden huts dating back to the early 1920s. It provided accommodation for over 200 school children who usually visited as part of a field study course. The centre had made substantial surpluses in past decades, but more recently the market had come to expect a better standard of accommodation than could be provided.

The youth centre at Newlands, some two and a half miles from Derwentwater, was closed in October 1988. Originally bought from CHA in 1913, Newlands had for many years been used for the provision of accommodation for 200 children. Multi-activity programmes had been introduced using some of the facilities at Derwent Bank for sailing and water sports, and Newlands had consistently paid its way. However since it was so close to Derwent Bank, it was not considered appropriate to convert it to an adult House.

Newlands, near Keswick is still run today as an activity holiday centre by the people who bought it from HF.

The future of Malhamdale was also under consideration. A number of options were considered but no action taken at that time.

Late in 1988 Thorns Hall in Sedbergh was purchased for opening the following Easter. Initially a small property, there were development possibilities to expand the capacity to between 35 and 40 people. It was felt to have considerable potential for walks in the Howgills, and the purchase of a property in a new area for the first time in sixteen years was considered a worthwhile achievement.

Changing Directions

The new Walking Department at Penrith also reviewed the way HF Holidays' walks are chosen and the system for providing Leaders with directions. Up to 1986 each centre had a Voluntary Field Assistant (VFA), recruited from the general leadership panel, who prepared a balanced two-week programme of walks. The directions were typed up in a narrative style in green books, and Leaders used these in conjunction with O.S maps. In the 1960s most centres also had the splendid picture maps on display, painted by Stan Duckles.

Now it was decided that each centre needed a team of two or three VFAs to provide an appropriate level of technical skill (eg navigation, risk assessment), written English, knowledge of the area and enthusiasm, and produce attractive and helpful walk descriptions to be sent to guests in an illustrated Programme of Walks.

At the same time a new tabular format was devised for the walks directions, which were laminated in plastic with accompanying O.S map extracts on which the route was highlighted. Risk assessments were also required and there was a new emphasis on making the walks more interesting for guests, by providing Leaders with background information (historical, botanical, geological etc) rather than just a route guide. Currently there are approximately 40 Field Advisors (as they are now known) in the UK with a similar number looking after resorts abroad.

Another development has been the Field Advisor/Leader Liaison File which is available in each House. All Leaders are required to read comments from previous Leaders about each walk they undertake, so that they can be aware of any new hazards since they or the Field Advisor last walked the route. The file also acts as a major prompt for Field Advisors to update the directions and enhance the quality of the walks.

Thorns Hall, Sedbergh, a 16th century manor house has the original wooden panelling in the public rooms

A small private school building (now known as Lanyons) adjacent to the property at St Ives was also purchased. The immediate benefit of this was that the mutual boundary could be demolished, the playground became a car park for the House, and the grounds were doubled in size. Indeed, within ten months of purchase the property was revalued at 50% more than its purchase price, although no work had been done on it.

The desire to reunite with CHA was still very strong in 1988 and the General Committee reported as follows:-

"Your Committee is now quite confident that the future of HF Holidays has been secured and that the coming years will see further improvement and strengthening. However, it will be difficult to generate the funds for major expansion without more guests and difficult to accommodate more guests without expansion; the demand for summer holidays already outstrips supply at many centres. Thus, if growth is to be more than gradual, we must consider a more radical approach to the problem.

"A logical solution is a merger with a kindred organisation and so the opportunity to discuss prospects of merger with the CHA during 1988 was fortunate. We found that many things united us and virtually none separated us so that progress towards an outline for agreement was initially rapid. The Annual General Meeting will be asked to approve further negotiations which, if successful, will lead to the convening of Special General Meetings of both organisations to deal with the necessary legal formalities.

"The present stage in the HF Holidays' recovery would be an ideal one for a merger along the lines envisaged. Most deficiencies on both the operational and the administrative sides of the organisation have been, or are on the point of being eliminated. Demand for holidays is buoyant and the level of guests' satisfaction high. All we lack is the size necessary to generate the funds needed for further growth. A merger with CHA would produce an organisation of such size and possessing a magnificent portfolio of properties offering almost ideal coverage of the UK's walking areas. Substantial benefits would be derived from the elimination of duplicated overheads so that holidays should represent even better value for money.

"Your Committee is pleased that, if the merger is approved HF Holidays will be bringing to the marriage a strong and growing operation which lacks nothing but the size necessary to generate the funds needed for further growth. Your Committee is confident that the merger is the best way to secure finest aspects of both HF Holidays and CHA for the generations to come."

It seemed at the time that the planned merger was almost a formality, but two years later the project was abandoned and both parties went their separate ways.

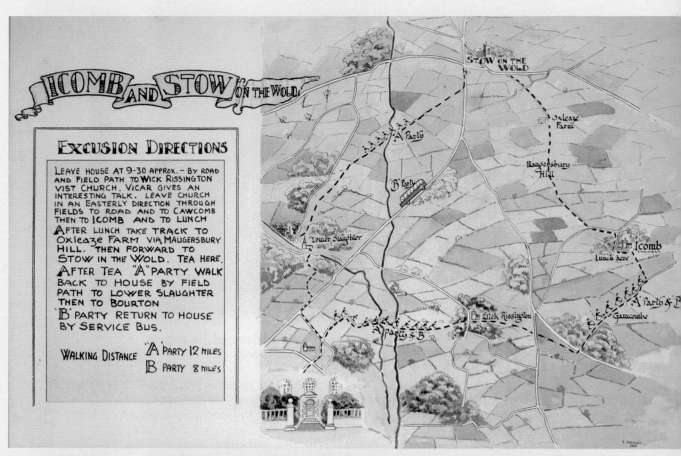

ICOMB AND STOW ON THE WOLD

EXCURSION DIRECTIONS

LEAVE HOUSE AT 9-30 APPROX. – BY ROAD AND FIELD PATH TO WICK RISSINGTON VIST CHURCH. VICAR GIVES AN INTERESTING TALK. LEAVE CHURCH IN AN EASTERLY DIRECTION THROUGH FIELDS TO ROAD AND TO CAWCOMB THEN TO ICOMB AND TO LUNCH

AFTER LUNCH TAKE TRACK TO OXLEAZE FARM VIA MAUGERSBURY HILL, THEN FORWARD TO STOW IN THE WOLD. TEA HERE.

AFTER TEA "A" PARTY WALK BACK TO HOUSE BY FIELD PATH TO LOWER SLAUGHTER THEN TO BOURTON

"B" PARTY RETURN TO HOUSE BY SERVICE BUS.

WALKING DISTANCE "A" PARTY 12 MILES
"B" PARTY 8 MILES

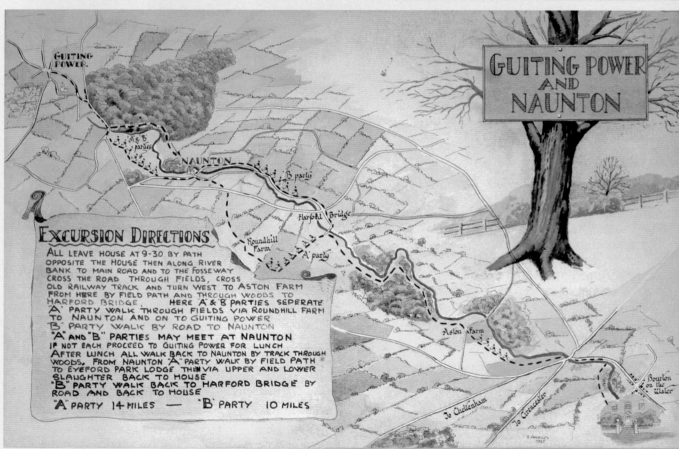

GUITING POWER AND NAUNTON

EXCURSION DIRECTIONS

ALL LEAVE HOUSE AT 9-30 BY PATH OPPOSITE THE HOUSE THEN ALONG RIVER BANK TO MAIN ROAD AND TO THE FOSSEWAY CROSS THE ROAD THROUGH FIELDS, CROSS OLD RAILWAY TRACK AND TURN WEST TO ASTON FARM FROM HERE BY FIELD PATH AND THROUGH WOODS TO HARFORD BRIDGE   HERE A & B PARTIES SEPERATE "A" PARTY WALK THROUGH FIELDS VIA ROUNDHILL FARM TO NAUNTON AND ON TO GUITING POWER "B" PARTY WALK BY ROAD TO NAUNTON

"A" AND "B" PARTIES MAY MEET AT NAUNTON IF NOT EACH PROCEED TO GUITING POWER FOR LUNCH AFTER LUNCH ALL WALK BACK TO NAUNTON BY TRACK THROUGH WOODS, FROM NAUNTON "A" PARTY WALK BY FIELD PATH TO EYEFORD PARK LODGE THEN VIA UPPER AND LOWER SLAUGHTER BACK TO HOUSE "B" PARTY WALK BACK TO HARFORD BRIDGE BY ROAD AND BACK TO HOUSE

"A" PARTY 14 MILES — "B" PARTY 10 MILES

Two examples of Stanley Duckles' delightful artwork, illustrating excursions from Bourton-on-the-Water in the 60s. No excuses for the odd spelling mistake!

Walk this way...

ICOMB, STOW-ON-THE-WOLD & WYCK RISSINGTON
A & B parties G5; C party G8
MAPS: 1" OS 144, 1¼" 163, 2½" OS SP 12/22
Walking distances: A party 14 m. B party 10 m.
C party 0-1 m. P.F. Public Footpath.

08.30 All parties get local bus at 09.40 to
Stow. 10.00 view church, stocks etc. toilets
near stocks. 11.00 Take road A436 E, fork R
and fork R again with car park on L go along
fenced stony road. Pass Nissen Hut and school
on L and large cut down tree trunk, through
stone pillars to cross roads, go straight on
bearing left past 'half moon' house on L. Come
to NO Through Road which enter, go downhill on
hard road, past Oxlease Farm GR 203244, then
uphill.

*Examples of the old and
new style walk directions
used by Leaders.*

WYCK RISSINGTON, OXFORDSHIRE WAY, ICOMB & STOW-ON-THE-WOLD

WALK NO. Bourton 7

DISTANCE: 12 km (7.5 miles)

ASCENT: 280 m (919 ft)

RETURN: PUBLIC TRANSPORT - Pick up point: Bus stop outside Pol. Stn.
at far end of square, Stow, 15.45 or 17.00
Return time: 15.55 or 17.10

MEDIUM WALK: Revised Autumn 1991
OUTWARDS: WALK FROM HOUSE - Set off time: 09.30
OTHER PARTIES - SW Party take Public Transport to
Moreton 10.00 or 11.15

MAPS: 1:50000 No 163
1:25000 SP 02/12 & SP 22/32

Dist Km	Ascent/ Descent	Time Mins	Directions	Comments	Grid Ref	Notes
					A 167206	
			From HOUSE (A) walk towards River Windrush, turn R downstream to PO, then L opp. PO along rd past Pulham's Bus Garage. Then turn R into Roman Way. After a few metres bear R along tarmac farm rd ENE for 25 m. At this point take path on R above rd between hedge & wall (172211). In 1st field keep hedge on L, in 2nd field cross diagonally (E) to gate & stile in far corner.	In 2 nd field the ditches & banks are part of an ancient encampment.		
2.7		65	Follow OW (Oxfordshire Way) waymarks with hedge on L in ENE direction, passing over plank bridges & thro' gates for 1.3 km to Wyck Rissington, emerging opp. POST BOX (B).		B 188219	1

In Harry's 20 years experience of HF Holidays every week has produced at least one memorable happening. Many of these have been notable enough to be wort repeating (although he has changed some names to save embarrassment).

The Rocket Romance

This all happened during a holiday at St Ives, where a nice young man in his early twenties, named Stephen, was very much in love with an equally nice young lady named Catherine.

They had adjoining single rooms on the first floor with a wonderful view out over the town and across the bay to Godrevy Head. A combination of this outlook, the warm weather, excellent company and the general ambience of a typical HF holiday had clearly provoked Stephen into action. He was obviously a very shy person, as was Catherine, but had decided he was going to press his suit, or plight his troth, and ask her to become his. Such innocence is so rare, especially amongst the young.

He confided all this to one of the Leaders on one of the walks early in the week and asked for some help. On the Thursday it was Catherine's birthday, and he had planned a little surprise. It transpired that Stephen was a development engineer with Banwell Fireworks and he had built a rocket. Not just any rocket, for this one had all sorts of special features, and he was going to impress Catherine with it and win her heart. Apparently they had been going out together for years, but the right moment had never presented itself to pop the question.

It was decided that the ceremony for *launching the rocket* would take place on the lawn in front of her window just before breakfast on Thursday morning. As many guests as possible would be invited, and at take off they would all spontaneously burst into "Happy Birthday dear Catherine, Happy Birthday to You".

All week the word went round, and it was a bit like *This is Your Life*. Everybody knew something, but nobody was saying anything.

On the appointed morning there must have been about thirty people all ready for the event, and Stephen produced his rocket. It was about six feet long or, more correctly, high, and the barrel piece at the top was about six inches in diameter. The stick was at least half an inch square, and would not go in the neck-hole of the largest bottle that could be found. It was finally wedged down the leg of an old Wellington boot that someone had left in the boot room and was aimed at a rakish angle towards Godrevy Lighthouse. Stephen had calculated that it might reach a height of one thousand feet, but he was a bit vague on this point.

Looking at the size of it, there was suspicion that any low aircraft could be in trouble, but the wind was in the right direction and it was pointing out to sea. The Leader appeared to be unofficially in charge of the firing, and as Stephen was clearly going to see it through, said to him, "OK Stephen, light it," "I've already lit it," he replied, "for about two minutes ago I saw my beloved peeking from the window."

A split second later there was a mighty whoosh and it was away, at about sixty degrees, out over the bay. Even in the bright morning sun there was a very clear vapour trail, and then, about a mile down range, there was one enormous thunderclap, followed by a huge ball of every different colour one could imagine, lasting about thirty seconds.

The gathering broke into a raucous "Happy Birthday, dear Catherine", and Stephen set off, flushed with success, to join her, and take his first steps towards matrimony.

The Chy Morvah, St Ives

Meanwhile, down at the harbour, St Ives had come alive. Men were running from all directions, putting on oilskins and rubber boots, then launching the lifeboat, which headed out to sea in great haste. It was probably the quickest launch ever, as the sea at the time was as calm as the proverbial mill pond. Not a wave, not a single ripple. Where they thought they were going, goodness only knows! Maybe it was just a coincidence, but there was a feeling that Stephen's rocket might have played some part in this occurrence. So, an apology was offered and accepted by the RNLI, after a suitable 'donation' had been negotiated, and four good things came out of this event.

1. The Lifeboat practice for the following Sunday was cancelled, allowing the crew to go fishing instead as was their want.

2. Banwell Fireworks never went into production with the 'Stephen Special'.

3. Most of the seagulls in the St Ives area disappeared for several weeks.

4. Catherine said "Yes!"

56

HF had an excellent year in 1989 with increased bookings, a high level of guest satisfaction and a strengthening financial position. Many newer Members rebooked and there was little spare capacity during peak periods. Improvement of House facilities, especially public rooms, had continued and much equipment was replaced.

A new lease was agreed with the National Trust for Holnicote House, Selworthy, for a further 25 years. This was extremely satisfying since it enabled future investments to be planned with confidence.

Following the Le Bettex experiment, 1989 saw the successful introduction of a new European programme of holidays. Departures were concentrated on ten locations with a longer holiday season at each. The holidays were based upon the UK House Party formula with at least two walking Leaders in residence. At most centres HF Holidays' guests were the only group in residence and so enjoyed sole use of the facilities. The results showed a high level of satisfaction, and the new approach enabled relationships with hotel owners to be built up over a period of time. This had benefits with regard to the welcome offered and the ambience, as well as an appreciation by the hotel of the long-term effects of providing customer satisfaction. Regular use of a particular hotel abroad also increased the level of knowledge amongst Leaders.

A new computerised reservations system provided improved service to guests. It enabled Reservations staff to provide a late booking service for many guests during the summer months, when a large number of last minute enquiries were received.

HF Holidays was featured on the popular TV programme *Wish You Were Here* featuring walking and golfing holidays at Alnmouth. After the programme HF Holidays received a large number of enquiries and subsequent bookings.

At the Bristol AGM in March 1988 a motion had been passed to *ban smoking as soon as possible in all HFs' Houses*. Significant progress was made in 1989 in the provision of no smoking areas. It was confirmed that there was to be no smoking in dining rooms and bedrooms and, in Houses with two or more lounges, one was designated non-smoking.

A surplus for the year was achieved after over £250,000 was spent on repairs and renewals to the fabric of the Houses. This reflected a substantial improvement on the financial position of previous years.

Our yardstick on prices, a week's holiday at Conwy, had risen to £169 with the transport costs an additional £13, an increase of 100% from 1979. The 'Special Interest' brochure had over 250 holidays on offer in the UK with another two dozen abroad. The most expensive holiday that year was two weeks' walking in Turkey, starting at Istanbul and described as "walks for the enjoyment of a great variety of evocative scenery, wild flowers and the eerie sense of atmosphere found in the remote parts of Turkey". Priced at £755, it included air fare from London and internal transport in Turkey.

The General Committee of the day summed up the decade as follows:-

"The position of the Society, although more secure than for many years, remains vulnerable to changes in the economic climate and to competitive pressures. The traumas of the early eighties bore testimony to the perils of failing to react to changing circumstances, particularly the aspirations of Members. We seek to combine the traditions which make HF Holidays special with the standard of facilities our newer Members have come to expect. In particular, we recognise the House Party as the essence of a true HF holiday, both in the UK and abroad."

Thus the 1980s ended on a cautiously optimistic note.

The Nineties

The opening of the decade saw many momentous changes. After a period of relative inactivity due to the merger discussions with CHA it was felt that necessary projects could no longer be delayed. Accordingly 1990 was extremely busy in every area of activity. Resources were stretched to the limit at times, but great success was achieved with continued (and increasing) support by holiday guests. Financial resources were generated to correct many long overdue areas of concern, and necessary capital was created by an operating surplus which supported further developments.

At the beginning of the year an opportunity presented itself with the discovery of a modest property at Dalwhinnie. Well situated (some 20 miles from Aviemore in the Central Highlands) The Grampian was purchased relatively cheaply, and with easy access to rail and road networks the accommodation offered an attractive holiday location in a new part of Scotland.

A programme of refurbishment was undertaken during the year so that it would be possible to open for the 1991 season. Built in 'Art Deco' style, the property seemed unusual for an HF Holidays' House, but prices reflected the low price paid for it.

Further south the Society had for a long time wished to re-enter the Brecon Beacons National Park. Since relinquishing the lease of Tregoyd House, Glasbury, in 1978 it had been felt that opportunities were being missed in this area. After an extensive search, Nythfa House at Brecon was purchased in October 1990. Nearly every room was en-suite and the House was ideally situated, being a short walk from the town centre and within sight of the cathedral. The area was said to be charming, reasonably uncrowded (except on the three known peaks) and within easy access of the Midlands and southern England.

A third new property was The New Inns at Alsop-en-le-Dale, just north of Ashbourne in the Derbyshire Peak District. A traditional hostelry for walkers on the Tissington Trail and one of the few establishments offering accommodation within walking distance of Dovedale, this House

The New Inns, Dovedale known today as Newton House

offered access to fine walking in the whole of the White Peak area.

The only remaining youth centre, Newfield Hall, Malhamdale, was a fine old building in a superb location. It was now an obvious choice for development, and an ambitious refurbishment and extension plan, comprising 32 en-suite bedrooms, began in the autumn of 1990.

Over half a million pounds was committed to this project, intended for completion in time for opening at Easter 1991. However, in January there was a major fire while the property was occupied by building contractors. The damage caused was so extensive as to warrant closure throughout the year and the House was only handed back by the contractors in November. Fortunately HF was adequately insured and received a further £500,000 towards the reconstruction project.

Early in 1991 it was decided to sell Loch Awe House, and it passed from HF's ownership in the last week of October. It had been a much-loved House, visited by approximately 2,000 people every year, and during the limited weeks it was open occupancy was extremely high. But because of the short opening season and high maintenance costs it had made substantial losses.

The Highest Point in Wales

Nythfa House, Brecon

I was a guest on one of the first weeks at Brecon in 1991 and a fellow guest on the same holiday will never be forgotten for several reasons. His name was Kenneth and he was a retired gyroscopic engineer who had been with British Aerospace for over forty years. A nicer man you couldn't wish to meet, but like many intelligent people he was a little bit odd at times.

We arrived together on Saturday, and the Leader who greeted us was delighted to observe that Kenneth had a violin case amongst his luggage. He was immediately signed up for the concert, and hadn't even been shown to his room. Such is the way with some Leaders.

Kenneth and I had the same interest in aeroplanes, and similar backgrounds in the aerospace industry, so we quickly became friends. We both preferred the short walks, and this is where the first story begins. Kenneth was careless where he put his feet down and consistently fell over. His reactions were sometimes a bit slow, so occasionally the first thing to hit the floor was his face. His wife, who always did the long walks, patched him up each night before dinner, but her first aid technique was not very good. Her standard repair job for a cut or abrasion was two elastoplasts in the shape of a cross. Apart from hands and elbows, and other places out of sight, these appeared on his forehead, nose, both cheeks and a small assortment all round his chin. Fortunately, some healed up as others appeared during the week, but at any one time there were at least two crosses on his face. Through it all he just smiled and said, "One of those things". His wife, who had known him longer than British Aerospace, just muttered quietly but unsympathetically something like "clumsy old devil" – but they were happy.

The second event happened quite early on, perhaps on the first or second walk, when during a coffee stop Kenneth produced from his rucksack what looked like an Ovaltine tin, and studied the lid intensely. "How high do you think we are?" he said. For a moment I thought he had something special in the tin, but he carried on, "What do you think is our current altitude?" I always carried a map in those days as I never fully trusted the Leaders, so I was able to tell him we were at approximately 700 feet. "That's very strange," he said, flicking the Ovaltine tin with his finger. "Are you sure?"

It transpired that this gadget was a homemade altimeter. Goodness knows what was inside, but on the lid was a needle, which was swinging gently to and fro around a crude dial with about twelve equally spaced notches on it, and the whole thing was held together with an elastic band. "What does your instrument indicate?" I asked, and without any hint of surprise he said, "22,000 feet – are you sure the map is correct?" He put it away saying, "It probably needs recalibrating," and I never saw it again.

The pièce de résistance came at the concert where Kenneth had volunteered to play the violin – surprise, surprise. His wife, whose name I can't remember, was going to accompany him on the piano, and when their time arrived she took her seat while he attempted to erect his music stand. Instead of the usual thing that just snaps open, this was a homemade version that he put together with nuts and bolts and a spanner. The audience were in fits, but nobody laughed out loud as nobody was sure if it was part of the act. Finally he was ready and said to his wife, "Give me an A, darling." Well she did, and he gave a rasp on the violin. The two notes were close, but not the same. "Again, darling." With the same result, but this time a little closer. I thought some of the audience would explode. Then Kenneth produced his masterstroke. Out of his pocket there appeared a tuning spanner and, lifting the lid of the ancient upright HF piano, he fiddled about inside the back. "Now try again, darling," and this time it was spot on. We were all amazed, and even more so when they proceeded to give us a ten-minute virtuoso performance, of professional concert standard. Thank goodness no one had laughed. They did a short encore, received rapturous applause, and the evening continued to its conclusion.

Afterwards, when most people had drifted off to bed, I went and played a few notes on the piano. I could not believe he had really tuned it to his violin. Not only that, in the middle C octave there were at least three notes that were now exactly the same!

Next day we all went home and I have never been back to Brecon. But since then in every House I visit, one of the first things I do is play the middle C octave on the piano. You never know, Kenneth might just have been one of the previous week's guests.

Fellowship House, Hendon

Another important sale that year was of 'Fellowship House', HF's Head Office at 142/146 Great North Way, Hendon. This had been purchased in the 1930s, was viewed with great affection by all staff, and engendered a friendly team spirit. But it was obvious that the working conditions for nearly 50 employees had degenerated to a point where they were rapidly becoming unacceptable. So in August everyone moved to leasehold offices some 3 miles away in Colindale. The Society then had the use of approximately 7,500 square feet of office space, recently refurbished on an 18 years lease. At a rental of under £10 per square feet this was felt to serve the needs of the Society adequately for the foreseeable future.

Continuing refinement and development took place in holiday programmes during 1991. A new programme of 'Leisure Breaks' was published to cater for a perceived demand for holidays "out of season" and of shorter duration.

Occupancy levels continued to rise and the year saw an increase in the number of guests taking holidays with the Society. The Abroad programme was particularly well supported despite difficulties in Yugoslavia during the middle of the year, and the background of the Gulf War during the early part of the year. For the first time a small programme of 'Worldwide' holidays was offered.

A detailed analysis of nearly 8,000 holiday questionnaires was undertaken at the end of the season. The results highlighted many useful pointers in the UK where further attention was needed both to buildings and also management performance.

1992 saw an even higher level of guest satisfaction, and a further strengthening of the financial position. In a year of changing property values HF Holidays applied its resources towards continued refurbishment rather than property purchase. Following the fire, Newfield Hall, was reopened completely refurbished and with all rooms en-suite. This magnificent House now stood proudly as the flagship of HF Holidays' properties.

The service guests received continued to improve through new and more efficient technology, including a computerised British Rail ticket service, a quick search facility for guest bookings, and a new computer facility for the Abroad Department to improve administration. New computer software in the UK Walking Department enabled better communication to Leaders and the closer matching of walking Leaders' abilities.

During the year 'Challenger Holidays' were introduced to cater for the very fit and more experienced walker. This had been well received and further developed for 1993. Holidays for 'singles' sold well and much interest was shown by the press in what was clearly a growing market.

The abroad programmes exceeded all expectations despite the turbulence in various parts of the world, and an assessment and training course for new abroad Leaders was introduced.

But although 1992 was a good year for HF, it will probably be remembered most for the tragic loss of the Chief Executive, Peter Brassey, who died in an accident on Sunday 2 August while walking in the French Pyrenees. He was 45.

Peter Chapman

Since joining HF in 1983 he had made an outstanding contribution to the success of the organisation and its fortunes.

Peter Chapman succeeded Peter Brassey, having for the previous seven years been the Deputy General Secretary, responsible for abroad operations.

In 1993 the Country Houses enjoyed increased occupancy, and guest satisfaction attained record levels. The financial position improved so much that HF was able to maintain high levels of investment in the upgrade and refurbishment of the properties. The walking programmes in both the UK and abroad saw excellent support from the guests. Special interest holidays maintained their popular appeal, and for the second year in succession HF Holidays won the *Daily Telegraph Reader Travel Award* as the "Best Activity Holiday Organiser".

Continuous quality improvement had become an integral part of the development of the Society. Leader training continued at a high level of activity. The first module for a Leaders' training manual was produced. Additional training courses for Leaders included First Aid, incident management, and communication. Leader performance was now being monitored based on guest questionnaires. A quality appraisal of 'Special Family holidays' was held, resulting in improvements to holidays and the assessment of Children's Activity Leaders. Children's holiday questionnaires were introduced, and enthusiastically completed and returned.

The property at Dalwhinnie had not attracted sufficient support and after only two years was closed. But in June contracts were exchanged for the purchase of Abingworth Hall, a superb property near Storrington in West Sussex.

In April, an 'Autumn in Britain' brochure, covering the period September to Christmas, was published and bookings from this helped strengthen the occupancy of Houses during what is often an excellent time of year for walking and other types of holiday interests. Guest bookings from North America, Australia and Europe also increased and helped to enrich the atmosphere of friendliness in HF Holidays' Houses.

The Grampian, Dalwhinnie

Christmas at HF Holidays

HF holidays are not only about spring, summer and autumn. For years there have also been traditional Christmas holidays in the UK Houses, which have always had a very special style, as described here by Leaders Jan and Dave Fullman, who led at Christmas for many years.

The House is all lit up. Christmas decorations are hung everywhere. In pride of place is the Christmas tree. Underneath the tree are three sacks marked 'Lady', 'Gentleman' and 'Either' ready to receive presents brought by guests to be distributed by Father Christmas.

The Leaders are gathered to welcome guests as they arrive. Some are recognised as old friends; some are new but they too will soon become friends. The Leaders (the cads!) are already plotting. "I've just spotted a possible Cinderella!" "See that chap? He doesn't know it yet but he could be one of the Ugly Sisters."

Once all the guests are safely gathered in, Christmas begins in earnest. After dinner they are advised by the Leaders of the various forthcoming festivities. More immediately will be the Christmas Eve Anthology which is a mixture of stories and poems from Dickens to Dylan Thomas, descriptions of customs (including some terrible cracker jokes!) and carols. Country dancing usually follows and everyone is looking forward to the big day.

It is 7.00am on Christmas morning. The Leaders, with various hangers-on who want to be part of the choir at this unearthly hour, sally forth to attempt to awaken guests around the House with fine renditions of Christmas carols. These are met with varying degrees of success, ranging from pennies, jelly babies or chocolate coins thrown out of bedrooms by apparitions in nightdresses or pyjamas, or comments through closed doors, the more polite of which is "Clear off!" After breakfast we get booted ready for the walk.

And so to lunchtime on Christmas Day. You are sitting on a rock on a mountain or fell, or maybe looking at the crashing waves from high on a coastal path. The rain or snow is soaking or freezing. While you try and warm your numbed fingers and stop the wet from trickling down your neck, you think of the millions of so-called normal folk sitting down to their Christmas Dinner. However, those soggy sandwiches taste really good in the open air, and the banter, chatting and laughter truly warms the very 'cockles of one's heart'. Ahhhh! But when you get back to the House and have a bath and change of clothes, you go down to the dining room to find that those bedraggled walking companions have been transformed into smartly dressed ladies and gents who sit down to evening dinner with its heaving Christmas fare. After a day's walk it is a feast

that has been well earned and is equally well enjoyed. This is a Christmas to be remembered. After dinner, fun and games, possibly more dancing and no television – Christmas how it used to be.

Boxing Day, another series of walks, followed by an equally sumptuous evening meal, and then the Pantomime. What would Christmas be without the Panto on Boxing Day? Men who in their working life could be a bank manager or a bus driver now become Ugly Sisters, 6' 1" tall, weight 14 stone, with moustaches, strutting their full bosomed stuff in high heeled shoes, slinky dresses and pink wigs. And we have glorious memories of slightly tipsy Fairy Godmothers and elegant Prince Charmings, sexy Cinderellas and even a lecherous Buttons.

What riotous laughter always accompanies both the rehearsals and the performance!

Come 6 o'clock every evening the lounge is packed for 'story time'. The Leader utters those immortal words "Are we sitting comfortably – then I'll begin" and carries on to read another story from Roald Dahl's book *Revolting Rhymes* (The most popular, with its infamous line "One eyelid flickers, she whips a pistol from her knickers", is his version of Little Red Riding Hood!).

Many guests leave after Boxing Day to be replaced by others. The rest stay on to enjoy more walks and evening activities – sketches, quizzes, chaotic games and more country dancing.

Christmas at HF Holidays is indeed a unique experience, and guests always leave with an extra suitcase – full of memories!

The Cast of Cinderella, Selworthy 1998. The Fairy Godmother later became the Lady Mayoress of a large town on the South Coast

*Craigside House, Swanage,
two adjacent Victorian Boarding houses,
knocked into one on the upstairs landing.
Very confusing until you got to know the layout!*

Early in 1995 a contract for the sale of Craigside House, Swanage was exchanged.

This followed confirmation that the car parking facilities in the grounds of the convent opposite were no longer available. Those guests who knew Craigside House would recall the immense difficulty in parking anywhere else near the House and the absence of reasonable public transport, made the decision to sell inevitable. The House was available to guests throughout the season, but would be sadly missed.

All the other properties continued to benefit from redecoration and improvement. Keeping 19 Country Houses in good repair was an increasingly expensive task and almost £1,000,000 was invested in 1995. A much needed conservatory extension at Derwent Bank was completed, and at Malhamdale work proceeded on a new dining room, extra single en-suite rooms and an indoor swimming pool.

Then in May the Society were delighted to unveil Castlebeigh House in Pitlochry, Perthshire. It was a stone built Victorian mansion set in three acres in an elevated position, with marvellous views of the town and mountains beyond.

The Activity Centres (Young Persons Safety Act) came into force on 1 August 1996. This said that "unless the operator providing the walks is licensed by the Authority, people under the age of 18 years must be accompanied by a parent or legal guardian on any walks on moorland or over 600 metres high, where help or ambulance access is more than half an hour away".

HF Holidays had always had a policy that young people under 14 years should be accompanied by a parent or legal guardian on its mountain and moorland walks, and so this new act only affected those between the ages of 14 and 17 years. Along with all other activity organisers, HF Holidays was discussing the requirements with the Licensing Authority and by the next summer hoped to be able to accept unaccompanied young people over 14 years on all walks. In the meantime, the 1997 Walking in Britain brochure was to list those walks on which restrictions for unaccompanied young people under 18 years would apply. Unfortunately this unsatisfactory situation was to continue for some years.

In 1997 the purchase of Larpool Hall near Whitby was announced. The hotel came into HF's possession in January 1998 and, after a period of hosting a number of banquets, conferences and weddings (booked in advance by the previous owners), it quickly became a firm favourite with guests wishing to visit Yorkshire's moors and coast.

1998 was a difficult year for the UK holiday trade as a whole, with hotel business down by an average of 15%. In this climate HF did well to register only a 5% drop in UK operations. However there was an equivalent increase in demand for holidays abroad with virtually all departures full. Many analysts believed the swing to abroad holidays was a temporary phenomenon, citing the strong pound, building society windfalls, the World Cup and the poor weather in Britain.

Castlebeigh House, Pitlochry opened in 1995.

Larpool Hall, Whitby

The Breakfast Special

When Scarborough closed, it was the passing of the evening trips to the Spa Theatre, or to the Alan Ayckborn, Stephen Joseph Theatre in the Round. Very sad.

However, there was immediately splendid compensation in the acquisition of Larpool Hall, Whitby, and among the many attractions of this lovely old building is the view from the bay window of the dining room. The guests have superb meals sitting at the table in the window, looking out over the valley and up the River Esk towards the moors. But the meal at the centre of this memorable happening had nothing to do with the vista, and everything to do with two ladies who sat down to breakfast on a Sunday morning in the late summer of 1998.

There was a fairly large group in the house from Birmingham, and these two ladies, of mature years and with strong black country accents, were just sitting there in the bay window when a nice young man came along to take their order. It was his first job since leaving school as a sixteen year old, his first day at work, and he was waiting on guests for the first time. He boldly walked up, cleared his throat, notebook and pencil at the ready, and in a broad Yorkshire accent said, "Allo, what are we having for breakfast like?"

The two ladies, who were both a little deaf, didn't hear him, but instead one of them asked the other what was on the menu. She studied the menu very carefully, and the following fiasco developed as she read out to her friend, "assorted fruit juices, cornflakes, bran flakes, weetabix, croissants, grapefruit and prunes". The young man started to write furiously, and when she paused at the end of the section it gave him a chance to catch up.

She continued, "boiled eggs, scrambled eggs, poached eggs, tomatoes, bacon, mushrooms, hash browns, baked beans, fried bread, and black pudding."

The medium party crossing the beck in Wheeldale. (Note the rain gear.) The author who was leading, is on the far left.

Off he went again with the look on his face showing more and more signs of incredulity. He stopped briefly a couple of times to look her up and down, but kept going to the end and dotted the 'i' in black pudding with a flourish.

Then came the 'coup de grâce'. After another short pause she added, "Oh and kippers!"

At that point the poor chap could not contain himself any longer. He somehow plucked up sufficient courage and said, "Would you like it all on the same plate?"

For a brief moment the ladies looked at each other, not appreciating what had happened. Then there was lots of laughter, but the poor lad was already disappearing towards the kitchen looking extremely embarrassed. Their merriment turned to consternation. Surely there could not be a plate big enough to cope with such an order, not even in Yorkshire. After a while, he came back empty handed to explain that there was no black pudding that morning. Thankfully it gave them the opportunity to correct the mistake, and they ended up with toast and marmalade.

At the end of the week it was observed that a certain lady put a very large donation into the staff box. But the next time she and her friend went to Whitby, the young man was no longer there. He had probably moved to another hotel, where the guests' appetites were not quite so large, tha knows!

'The Mysterious Affair at Styles' although set in East Anglia, was mostly written while Agatha Christie was staying at Moorlands.

Also in 1998 the AGM approved the modernisation of the Society's Rules (including the re-naming of the General Committee as Board of Directors) and the purchase of Moorlands, near Haytor, in the Dartmoor National Park was announced. After a period of refurbishment, it was opened in early spring 1999, and promised to mirror the success of Larpool Hall in an area which had needed an HF presence for many a long year. With beds for 63 guests, huge public rooms and magnificent views, the House was ideal for guests looking for something different.

During 1999, the Board and Executive devoted considerable time to preparing the ground for a strategic review. Whilst happy with HF Holidays' development in recent years – both in terms of financial performance and the service provided to guests and Members – the Board were aware of increasing competitive pressures on the one hand, and new opportunities in the market, especially for walking, on the other.

In the decade, turnover had increased from £5.5m to £12.8m. A significant operating surplus had been generated every year and a dividend of at least 3% paid to Members. The number of shareholders had risen from 22,914 to 26,032, each one now with a minimum shareholding of £25.

Our week's holiday at Conwy was £344 by the turn of the century, but the excursion transport was now included in the holiday price. The Special Interest brochure contained over 500 holidays, twice the number of ten years before. The most expensive holiday in 1999 was in the Worldwide brochure, where three weeks walking and sightseeing in New Zealand cost £3,699.

Management Matters

The location and spread of HF Holidays' UK Houses makes it difficult for their Managers to share ideas, so an annual conference is held in January, as soon as practical after the Christmas and New Year period holidays, for discussion, training and development. Since the mid 90s, with the increasing focus on health and safety legislation, it has also ensured that HF follows good business practice and statutory requirements.

The Conference usually lasts four days, and rotates around the UK Houses, so that most Managers will have the honour, (or challenge) of entertaining their colleagues. The Chief Executive, Heads of Department from both the London and Penrith offices and two or three Board members also attend, along with representatives from outside companies to present or support topics on the agenda.

High on the list of subjects discussed is guest satisfaction and the quest for continuous improvement in the hotels, and on the last night at the 'Conference Dinner' the annual awards are presented. These are based on a combination of the guests' holiday questionnaires and budgeted cost achievements. They include 'Friendliness of Staff', 'Most Improved House', and 'Best Food', with the top award being 'House of the Year'.

John & Jan Croxford collect the House of the Year award for Glen Coe in 1995.

Another important development has been the decision to seek the national standard of Investor in People. This requires a commitment to the training of all employees up to the highest possible levels, and is similar to the kite mark standard for manufacturing industry. It involves a rigorous and lengthy examination by a national assessor of every aspect of the Society's operations, concentrating in particular on the way the company invests in the development of its staff and Leaders. It was first awarded to HF Holidays in 1994, and the 'Investor in People' logo is now proudly displayed on all our literature.

INVESTOR IN PEOPLE

In 1996 the range and diversity of the holiday products was reflected in the choice and number of brochures that were available.

All in the family

T A Leonard was a true pioneer. In the late 1890s he championed the rights of women to join his holidays. As he explained in *Adventures in Holidaymaking*, "We helped to rationalise women's dress, for there was no comfortable tramping and climbing in the absurd garments they are supposed to wear. At first it was a shock to see our girls start out in sensible outdoor clothes."

Then in 1934 he turned his attention to children, with the opening of the first Family Centres at Marske, on the North Yorkshire coast, and Milford, on the Solent. This was a response to requests from young couples who had met on HF, subsequently married, and now had young families. "We shall probably find it difficult to make such centres pay," admitted Leonard, "but the hope is that by showing the way others will follow."

HF has actively promoted family holidays ever since. After the Second World War, Tywyn, on Cardigan Bay, joined the list of Family Centres, where families were given priority during the school holidays, and then Colwyn Bay in North Wales in the 60s. Here's what one Member recalls of his time as a Centre Secretary there.

I have many happy memories, but one stands out. It concerns a 5 year old boy called Edward, who was the youngest of five siblings, but by no means the shyest. Every morning after breakfast, when I was preparing for the walk in the small office (which doubled as a kind of tuck shop), four chubby fingers would appear over the lip of the counter, for Edward was too small to be visible on the other side, and a cheeky voice would call out, "Anything free?"

After a few days of saying "No", I had an idea. "Listen, Edward," I said, "if you get to the top of the

An Easy Walk group in the 90s at the Wishing St near Ventnor, Isle of Wight.

mountain today you can have a free Trebor Chew tomorrow." "OK," said the voice, and the fingers disappeared. What I hadn't said was that the "mountain" was Snowdon, so I thought there was no danger of having to pay up! But Edward confounded me, for he climbed Snowdon unaided via the PYG track that day - certainly the only 5 year old I've ever led up there. So next morning there was a grand presentation at breakfast. Not only a Trebor Chew (price 1d), but also a cloth sunburst "HF" badge (retailing at 2/6), for his mum to sew on the back of his rucksack.

But that wasn't quite the end of the story. For after breakfast, as I sat in the secretary's office basking in my own munificence, the chubby fingers re-appeared and the cheeky voice asked "Anything else free?"

The walking programmes at these Family Centres were modified to include a "pushchair party", and the Wednesday "off-day" often featured children's sports, with obstacle, egg and spoon, three-legged

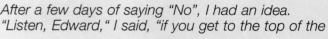

The "pushchair party" lunching by Llyn Crafnant in the 60s

nd sack races. There were lso strict bedtime rules. Children under 9 had an early igh tea and were in bed by .00pm; those from the ages f 9 to 12 joined dinner at .30pm, but went to bed efore the evening activities tarted at 9.00pm; and the rst year a young teenager was allowed to witness these was a true rite of passage!

n the 70s the rules relaxed. Children of all ages were now welcomed at any centre, with pecial Family Weeks at a wider range of locations, mountain nd moorland as well as coastal. These continue oday and have proved a real investment, for many dults return to HF in middle-age because of their appy memories of family holidays. There are also ow "Family Plus" weeks for parents (and randparents) with babies and toddlers, and Family Adventure" holidays, where parents go walking while their children enjoy a range of things ke canoeing, abseiling, archery and rock climbing. There's also a "Family Cycling" holiday at Dovedale.

But walking remains the most popular activity, and ne of the key attractions is that there are three sometimes four) different walks each day, so that families can split up if they wish, each member choosing according to their ability. As we've seen, for some years this freedom was frustrated at mountain centres by the Children's Activity Centre legislation, leaving disappointed 17 year olds who couldn't climb Great Gable because neither parent felt up to accompanying them! But in 2006 after long negotiation and considerable Leader re-training, the old freedom was restored, so once again unaccompanied children from age 14 can choose whichever walk they like.

Marske, 1949.
The Member who went on to be the Centre Secretary at Colwyn Bay is crawling under the leftmost chair!

Damp Doings on the Down

A few years ago HF Holidays provided all Houses with survival tents to be carried by Leaders on all walks at all times. They are very lightweight and roll up into a small pack, easily carried at the bottom of a medium-sized rucksack. Coloured fluorescent red and yellow, they can be seen for miles, and although designed for two or three people can accommodate a few more. The idea is that you open up the tent, stand in a small group facing each other, lift the tent over all your heads, pull it down your back and then sit down. Your heads become the human tent poles and it works very well.

Ever resourceful, I pressed it into a different kind of use one very wet day in 1996 at Abingworth. I was in charge of the Long party that day, and the walk in question starts in the village of Steyning and climbs out onto the South Downs. There is then a large circle to negotiate, taking in the tops of several Iron-Age forts, before visiting Chanctonbury Ring and dropping back down into Steyning, hopefully in time for a pot of tea before catching the coach back to Abingworth Hall.

Fortunately there were only eight people in the party that day, and why this was fortunate will become apparent shortly. It was one of those days when the weather was sunny and rather warm, but then a sudden heavy shower would have us reaching for our waterproofs. By lunchtime the rain gear had been on and off at least half a dozen times, and a few of the short, sharp showers had been ignored altogether. Everyone in the party was wearing shorts, and it was quite pleasant, especially on the tops of the hills, to brave the elements for a few moments every now and then.

At lunchtime we all went to the pub in Findon, which was a mistake. Findon is one of the centres of the horse racing fraternity in this part of the country, and there was a celebration taking place of a recent big race winner. Somehow we got involved and so left the pub

a little behind schedule. We had climbed back to the top of the Downs, heading for home, when it started to rain with a vengeance. This was no shower, but instead of getting out the already soggy waterproofs, we moved immediately to *Plan B.*

Sometime during the previous year I had sheltered under the survival tent very successfully in a rainstorm. It was on Dartmoor, and I found that by all standing together you could get at least twelve people underneath, or inside, at the same time. With only eight people it was so much easier, and as the trail up on the South Downs is quite wide we discovered that we could actually continue the walk under the tent. With a little practice, all taking the same length of stride and using the air hole as a forward periscope, we were able to carry on regardless of the elements towards Steyning.

At first there were no other walkers up there but eventually, and I suppose inevitably, another small group came into sight, going in the opposite direction and using more traditional waterproof gear, but obviously very wet. By comparison, the HF group were all remarkably dry. In fact they had started to generate some heat, and when they stopped there were wisps of steam escaping from the

Abingworth Hall, Abingworth

air holes and from underneath the canopy.
In spite of the conditions both parties stopped
and the following banter took place.

Group outside:	"Where are you from?"
Group inside:	"We are from the planet OG."
Group outside:	"Where is your spaceship?"
Group inside:	"In the car park at Steyning."
Group outside:	"Where do you want to go?"
Group inside:	"We wish to speak with your leader, Blair."
Group outside:	"He lives a long way away in the city of London, but you are going in the right direction."
Group inside:	"We thank you, and had better be off then."

And with that we immediately fell into step and marched away leaving the other group wet and helpless.

On the way down into Steyning it was quite slippery and the rain had abated a little, so the tent came off and we descended with the appropriate amount of safety and decorum. On reaching the outskirts however, down came the rain again, so on went the cover and we completed the walk with intent, as it were!

Fortunately Steyning High Street was almost empty and although we stopped outside a café we resisted the temptation to go in. So this red and yellow thing, with sixteen hairy legs, short nose and a hump on its back (that was the back marker's rucksack) made it safely back to the sanctuary of the bus, and home.

Next day it was fully expected that the local newspaper would carry the headline - *"Aliens Land in Sussex".*

The 21ˢᵗ Century

The year 2000 saw interest from North America increase substantially following the introduction of the HF Holidays' website and in the UK there was a further improvement in occupancy levels, with particular demand for short breaks in the early and late parts of the year.

Worldwide holidays set a new booking record, reflecting excellent support for the unique policy of offering a choice of walks each day. A number of new destinations were introduced, supported by departures from Manchester and other northern airports.

During the year advertising was again increased in the national and regional press, specialist walking magazines, women's magazines and others. There were poster campaigns on London Underground stations, and contact with the media and press through radio interviews and editorials. The internet played its part too, with many e-mails a day received from the USA, Australia, continental Europe as well as the UK.

The highest level of demand for brochures ever was recorded. As part of the new development, the HF Holidays' name was redesigned to give a more up-to-date image and each holiday brochure had a 'new look' logo to reflect the type of activity being offered.

During 2000 Coram Court at Lyme Regis in Dorset was sold because of concern for its long-term viability.

Late in 2000 the *Countryside and Rights of Way Act* came into force. This new legislation created a new right of public access to some 4 million acres of mountain, moorland, heath, downland and registered commonland in England and Wales. For HF Holidays, this was a real step forward, but just as new rights were given by law, old ones were temporarily removed by the most damaging issue to affect HF since World War Two.

The calamity occurred in late February 2001 with the outbreak of foot and mouth disease in Northumberland. It quickly spread around the country, and in no time at all, HF was battling to find somewhere to walk that wasn't closed down. The international and domestic markets

Coram Court, Lyme Regis opened in 1919. One of the interesting features was a fireplace and chimney breast in the centre of the dining room/ballroom. When the House was full, the guests had to dance around this obstacle, and while some thought it was an inconvenience, others felt it enhanced the atmosphere of the evenings.

all but collapsed. By April seven of the Country House hotels were closed for the season, the other UK properties surviving on low occupancy levels. Many staff were out of work or on reduced times or salaries, although often working even longer hours. To try to obtain some redress for our financial losses, a number of meetings took place with Ministers, and there was much publicity for our cause. But the government had turned its face away from British tourism, and we were no exception.

There is often a brighter aspect to a crisis, and, in HF's case, the abroad business performed extremely well. Demand for walking holidays there rose and the capacity of a number of holidays was increased. As a result, many guests were still able to enjoy their annual walking holidays by crossing the channel. In the meantime in the UK an alternative programme called 'Give Us A Break' was quickly developed and proved popular. A mixture of walking and sightseeing, it was to be repeated in 2002.

There is no doubt that tourism in the UK, and walking holidays in particular, suffered great damage in 2001 from the Foot and Mouth epidemic. But later in the year there were signs that walking as a holiday activity would not just recover but grow, as stressful lifestyles demanded more rest and recreational opportunities.

Thurlestone Sands House, South Devon,

During the year, a new holiday programme entitled 'Classic Wanderer' was introduced offering freedom, flexibility and choice for the independent walker. Holidays to France and Spain were available with more destinations planned as the programme developed. Also new in 2001 was a much expanded programme of gentle holidays for cross-country skiing, snow-shoeing and winter walking in countries throughout Europe and Scandinavia under the 'Winter Experience' banner.

With so many Houses closed it was decided early on to take advantage of the opportunity by further investing in our properties. The redevelopment at Derwent Bank was completed during the winter months, and a splendid new spa pool at Larpool Hall, Whitby was ready by April.

Then in September 2001 a second event took place that would have a substantial impact on guest numbers. The attack on the World Trade Centre in New York led to far fewer US guests visiting HF Holidays' Houses in the next couple of years.

The British Tourist Authority reported that tourism into the UK from abroad in 2002 was down about a fifth compared to pre-2001 levels, whilst domestic holiday take up was beginning to recover. As the major provider of walking and special interest holidays in the country, HF was more affected than many other holiday operators, but bookings did come back in 2002 (who would miss an HF holiday unnecessarily?) and although they were about 15% lower than pre-2001 levels, some holidays, such as Classic Trails and Long Distance Walking holidays, enjoyed high demand.

The longer-term strategy to broaden the base of the organisation had a significant success early in 2002, when the acquisition of 'Anglo Dutch Cycling' holidays brought a new dimension to HF. Anglo Dutch operated in a number of countries in Europe, providing group and individual holidays. Cyclists share a love of the countryside and it was planned to provide many new cycling holidays in Britain and in Europe in future seasons.

Early in the year, a decision had been taken to close and sell Thurlestone Sands House in Devon. The House required heavy investment in excess of its market value and the Board took the view that investment in the remaining group of properties was a better option.

At the AGM held in Harrogate in March 2003, the President paid tribute to two Vice Presidents who had passed away. Sir Peter Pain had been President from 1977 to 1983. A High Court Judge and Chairman of the Race Relations Board Conciliation Committee, he had been an outstanding Chairman at the AGMs. Chris Brasher was an Olympic gold medallist, who went on to found the London Marathon and the British Orienteering Federation, as well as the successful Brasher Boot Company. They would both be greatly missed.

After excellent results for ten years or so, the last three years had been something of a shock to the system. The domestic and international upheavals more or less ruled out good financial results, but it was encouraging that the quality of the operation and the friendliness and efficiency of the staff remained unaffected, and the company did break even in 2002 and 2003.

Social evenings were part of the HF formula from the very start. For instance in the 1920s guests were advised:

1. *There will be discussions in the evenings on topical subjects of a non-controversial nature.*

2. *There may be folk dancing in the style of Cecil Sharpe, and possibly a short one act play.*

3. *The common room entertainment at all Houses closes at 10.30pm.*

4. *It is expected that guests will be in their own bedrooms and that absolute quiet will be observed after 11.00pm.*

By the end of the 1990s the strict bedtime rule had long since disappeared (as had the one act play readings) but the Evening Entertainment Programme was still an essential part of a good HF holiday. To provide this, each Leader would bring along some ideas, and the leadership team would put together a selection of activities for the week. There was often no specific structure to the programme, but it would usually include country dancing, a whist drive, a guest speaker, a quiz and, towards the end of the week, a concert.

The success of the evenings, and particularly the concert or Ceilidh, was down to the organisational ability of the Leaders, and the active participation (and often entertainment skills) of the guests.

However in 2000 it was decided to adopt a more structured approach, and capture and develop the best ideas for an evening programme. There were several meetings over the next couple of years where a group of more experienced Leaders spent time exchanging views on what constituted an enjoyable evening, and the project was co-ordinated by an expert in group entertainment. The result was a detailed manual of best working practices, which was then issued to all Leaders.

It was from these sessions that the new title 'Evening Options' was derived, and a more professional presentation style developed. Computer-generated posters are now created by the Leaders for each holiday, using a CD specially produced for HF Holidays. Gone are the days when the quality of the posters was dependent on the artistic merit of the Leaders! However, as the Penzance example from 1958 shows, the programme content has remained largely unchanged, which is a testament to the durability of the HF formula.

Remember

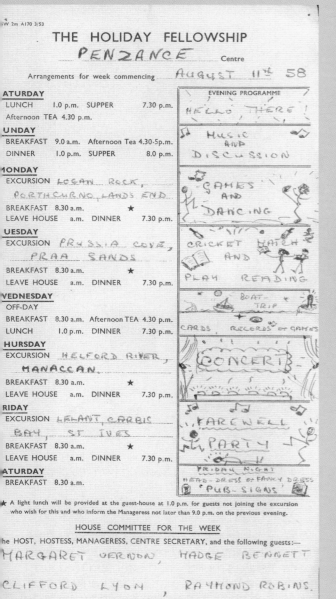

THE HOLIDAY FELLOWSHIP

PENZANCE Centre

Arrangements for week commencing **AUGUST 11th 58**

SATURDAY
LUNCH 1.0 p.m. SUPPER 7.30 p.m.
Afternoon TEA 4.30 p.m.

SUNDAY
BREAKFAST 9.0 a.m. Afternoon Tea 4.30-5p.m.
DINNER 1.0 p.m. SUPPER 8.0 p.m.

MONDAY
EXCURSION LOGAN ROCK, PORTHCURNO, LANDS END
BREAKFAST 8.30 a.m. ★
LEAVE HOUSE a.m. DINNER 7.30 p.m.

TUESDAY
EXCURSION PRUSSIA COVE, PRAA SANDS
BREAKFAST 8.30 a.m. ★
LEAVE HOUSE a.m. DINNER 7.30 p.m.

WEDNESDAY
OFF-DAY
BREAKFAST 8.30 a.m. Afternoon TEA 4.30 p.m.
LUNCH 1.0 p.m. DINNER 7.30 p.m.

THURSDAY
EXCURSION HELFORD RIVER, MANACCAN.
BREAKFAST 8.30 a.m. ★
LEAVE HOUSE a.m. DINNER 7.30 p.m.

FRIDAY
EXCURSION LELANT, CARBIS BAY, ST IVES
BREAKFAST 8.30 a.m. ★
LEAVE HOUSE a.m. DINNER 7.30 p.m.

SATURDAY
BREAKFAST 8.30 a.m.

EVENING PROGRAMME
HELLO THERE!
MUSIC AND DISCUSSION
GAMES AND DANCING
CRICKET MATCH AND PLAY READING
BOAT-TRIP
CARDS RECORDS or GAMES
CONCERT
FAREWELL PARTY
FRIDAY NIGHT HEAD-DRESS or FANCY DRESS 'PUB-SIGNS'

★ A light lunch will be provided at the guest-house at 1.0 p.m. for guests not joining the excursion who wish for this and who inform the Manageress not later than 9.0 p.m. on the previous evening.

HOUSE COMMITTEE FOR THE WEEK
The HOST, HOSTESS, MANAGERESS, CENTRE SECRETARY, and the following guests:—
MARGARET VERNON, MADGE BENNETT
CLIFFORD LYON, RAYMOND ROBINS.

Programme of walks and evening entertainment from week commencing 11 August 1958

For instance country dancing remains one of the favourites with guests, probably because it fits HF Holidays' culture of walking and talking during the day, dining together as a group, then sharing active enjoyment in the evening.

One other essential ingredient for many guests is a competition. This applies not only to team quiz evenings but also to weekly tournaments of table tennis, croquet, or putting, or the daily challenge of finding the roundest pebble or find the most unusual object on the walks, (this last being a big favourite on Family Weeks).

Another popular event is a 'Caption Competition' in which a photograph or picture is displayed, and guests are invited to add a humorous or edifying caption.

At the end of the week the Leaders offer a 'fabulous' prize, which often turns out to be a small bag of sweets, or some other inexpensive bauble.

*Winning caption:
"This had better be the
last flipping hill."*

*Winning caption:
Synchronised
bird spotting*

HF Holidays celebrated its 90th anniversary during 2003. Many Members enjoyed specially reduced-price holidays and all guests were able to benefit by the introduction of 'Many Happy Returns' loyalty discounts for repeat bookings. Group guests had their own special scheme, giving increasing levels of discount for repeat bookings over the years. Both of these schemes proved popular and were to continue.

The exceptional weather in July, August and September brought an upsurge in bookings for UK holidays, and the overall picture was one of steady improvement in holiday quality, good value for money and new holiday development. The global reach of the programme was exemplified by high demand for the new Barbados and Tasmania holidays, amongst others.

During the year HF Holidays became a member of the European Ramblers' Association, an organisation which promotes the interest of walkers through organisations in countries throughout Europe. It was also the main sponsor of the Isle of Wight Walking Festival, which attracted around 15,000 walkers to the island, many of them visiting Freshwater Bay House. The company exhibited for the first time at the Outdoors Show in Birmingham, and in August there was participation in an in-store promotion operated in conjunction with Cotswold Outdoor stores. Late in the year, the 200,000 readers of the Yorkshire Evening Post were treated to a special supplement on walking holidays in Yorkshire exclusively sponsored by HF Holidays, there were also features on HF Holidays in Country Walking Magazine, and a number of other health and lifestyle publications.

As a result 2004 brought increases in the number of guests taking holidays with more bookings in all programme areas and much excitement was generated by the plan to bring all walking holidays together into one brochure with a totally new design.

A basic rule for back-markers – always keep up with the party!

"Walking Holidays 2005" was published at the end of September, and received huge support for its clarity, simplicity and attention to detail. It promised to be "the natural and only choice for anyone seeking a walking holiday anywhere in the world."

So from now on there would be just three main publications to cover 'Walking', 'Cycling' and 'Inspirations'. This represented a major change from the brochure policy since 1996.

In 2005 a fine summer saw late booking in the UK whilst European and Worldwide bookings achieved new high levels. The new Self-Guided Walking programme grew strongly and cycling holidays in Europe were again popular. The strategy of spreading risk across walking and other activity areas was working well.

Guide to a good loo!

Harrington House, Bourton-on-the-Water

As we've seen, 2001 was not a very good year for HF Holidays in the UK. The foot and mouth outbreak meant that in some areas the walking season never got started. But it was not all doom and gloom. One of those amazing coincidences occurred that would not have come about but for the inventiveness needed to deal with the foot and mouth situation. The subject is toilets, and in particular the public toilet in the car park in the village of Broadway in the Cotswolds.

One of a Leader's briefs is to have detailed knowledge of all the public toilets on all the walks they cover - not only their whereabouts, but their potential cleanliness and, believe it or not, availability for use. A typical instance of availability, or lack of it, is the public toilet in Abbey Terrace in Winchcombe. This is ideally positioned, in that it's right at the start and / or finishing point of all the walks that feature in this attractive Cotswold town. Unfortunately it is not always open and, when locked, there appears on the door a very smart notice to the effect that "The Key can be obtained from the Book Shop in the High Street." On one holiday this so incensed two lady guests that they immediately set off to sort things out. After half an hour when they hadn't returned, the group went to find them, and in the book shop were redirected to the Town Hall, where they had gone to remonstrate with the Clerk of the Council. Everyone reconvened at the convenience (no pun intended), to start the walk about an hour behind schedule, but the world was a much better place to live in, and these particular toilets have never been locked since.

Meanwhile, back to the public toilet in Broadway car park! Some new walks had been introduced at Bourton-on-the-Water in the mid nineties and one had been planned to finish at Broadway. The town had installed a new car park at about the same time and pride of place was reserved for a state-of-the-art public convenience with an attendant named Alf. Naturally the finish of our walks is at Alf's establishment, and there is always a friendly greeting, an invitation to sign the visitors' book, hot water, real towels, fresh flowers etc, etc.

Alf's fame spread, and Gloucestershire Council were so pleased they entered the Broadway car park public convenience for the 1997 BOTTY Award. (This is The British Toilet of the Year, but someone has turned the letters round into a more appropriate acronym.) Anyway, they came second that year and second again in 1998, but in 1999 and 2000 they got the top prize and all the accolades that go with it, including a write-up in the Good Loo Guide. Naturally we were delighted that one of our walks finished at such a famous landmark and were all hoping that 2001 would be a treble or 'hat trick' year, but sadly it was not to be. For some reason the Broadway car park public convenience never even got a mention, and there the story would have ended, but for a remarkable coincidence, as follows.

Due to the foot and mouth difficulty, HF Holidays curtailed the walking programme in 2001 and introduced alternative holidays called Give us a Break. This involved visiting those areas of the countryside where limited access was still allowed, such as some stately homes, Warwick Castle, canal towpaths and some parts of arboretums. For instance at Abingworth we were able to use the south coastal paths from Bognor Regis right along to Brighton, and one walk in particular started in Littlehampton and finished at Worthing, with the pick up point right by the pier.

Now the public toilets on the south coast are generally considered to be towards the top end of the market, in contrast to the state of some of its beaches. (When we used to walk the coastal paths from the House at Lyme Regis the ladies' public convenience by the weir in West Bay was recognised as one of the finest in the whole south of England. All stainless steel and padded seats, and a basket for used hand towels.)

But we were still surprised, on completing our walk to Worthing Pier, to find a huge notice outside the fairly ancient public convenience proclaiming that these premises had been awarded the BOTTY prize for 2001. By an amazing chance we had come across the very establishment that had ruined Broadway's run of success. On investigation it was not apparently obvious why this had come about. No fresh flowers, no visitors' book, and no friendly greeting in a local dialect. They were very clean for such a busy place, but suspicions of collusion were in the minds of those of us that know a thing or two about what constitutes a really good loo!

In fact, when comparing the Broadway car park convenience with the Worthing Pier convenience, the words of T S Eliot come to mind, when he talked of 'dissociation of sensibility' and 'objective correlation' when comparing the old with the new.

But then, T S Eliot is an anagram of TOILETS.

Towards the end of 2005 the Board of Directors decided to sell Castlebeigh House, Pitlochry and to commence a new programme of development in the remaining Country Houses. It was also announced that there was now a satisfactory alternative to the original House at Swanage and holidays would commence there in the 2006 season.

So we reach the end of "The HF Holidays Story" - for the time being! As you'll see from the map at the end of the book, well over 100 UK centres have appeared in the brochures since 1913, and there are now hundreds more European and worldwide destinations on offer, with the list of 'Inspirations' ever more varied. Turnover has reached £16m, and guest numbers, despite national and international disasters, have steadily increased.

For the future there are exciting new building developments at two of our oldest houses, Alltshellach in Scotland and Bryn Corach in Wales, which of course is where the story began, and it's appropriate that the extra public rooms there will include a permanent home for the Heritage Collection, which has provided the illustrations for this book.

And what of the cost of our Conwy week? In 2007 it has reached £533 (remember, it was 37/- in 1913), but that's still in line with Leonard's ambition to provide an all-in holiday for the average weekly wage.

More important perhaps that we re-affirm the words of his favourite hymn (No. 37 in Songs o Faith, Nature and Fellowship), which express so beautifully the essence of a good HF holiday

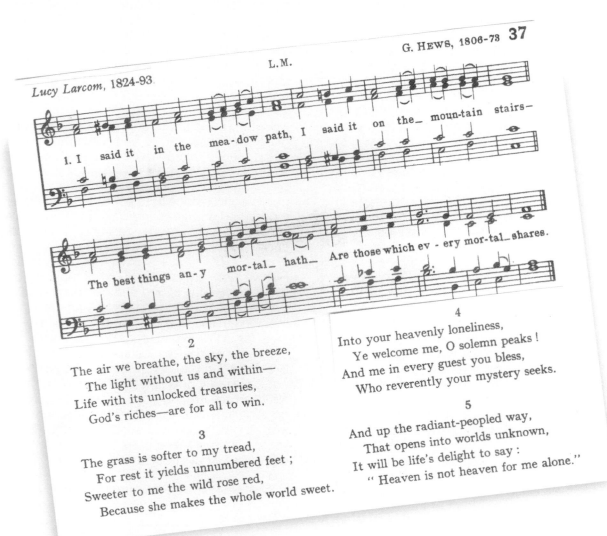

Coming soon…

A conservatory for Conwy

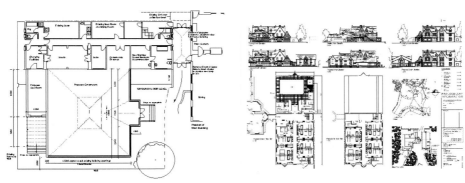

More bedrooms and a swimming pool for Glen Coe

Index of UK Locations
owned or leased since 1914

Where next?

As befits a walking organisation HF Holidays has never stood still. At any one time there have rarely been more than twenty houses owned by HF Holidays in the UK. But their location has constantly changed as the years have passed, to ensure our guests always get the best in accommodation in the finest countryside. Wonder where the 121st will be?

The
story of hfholidays
by Harry Wroe

ISBN 0-9555139-0-1

Author: Harry Wroe
Editorial Team: David Brown, Erica Looney,
Laura Sims, Chris Steel
Cartoonist: Ron Fountaine
Design: Gail D'Almaine for
Printers Incorporated Ltd
Print & Production: Printers Incorporated Ltd

ISBN 0-9555139-0-1

9 780955 513909 >

better walking altogether

hfholiday

Stage **1**

Schofield&Sims

Sound Practice 3

Practising phonics

eopar

ee

leaves

le me pe he

sh__p

propeller

was_

_n_

Name

Sound Practice Book 5

Sound Practice is a series of five workbooks
by Andrew Parker and Jane Stamford.

Sound Practice Book 1   978 07217 0862 1
Sound Practice Book 2   978 07217 0863 8
Sound Practice Book 3   978 07217 0864 5
Sound Practice Book 4   978 07217 0865 2
Sound Practice Book 5   978 07217 0866 9

Notes for the Teacher

This book gives practice in initial blends, end blends and digraphs and introduces the magic 'e'.

Exercises involving missing words are included and the book also gives scope for colouring the pictures.

To eliminate the need for written instructions, which often present a greater problem to children than the exercises themselves, pencil 'signs' (✐) have been introduced to indicate where the children must start to work and to copy the examples given.

When they have completed each page, children should read aloud their work to the teacher.

978 07217 0866 9

First printed 1981
Twenty sixth impression 2012

Schofield & Sims

Printed in England by Wyndeham Gait Ltd., Grimsby.
Cover design & illustration by Curve Creative, Bradford.